ICE-BREAKERS

and

THE ICE-BREAKER
HERSELF

by

EDNA GEISTER

Author of "It Is to Laugh"

NEW YORK
GEORGE H. DORAN COMPANY

PREFACE TO ICE-BREAKERS

THIS collection of games and stunts has been prepared for the express purpose of meeting the many requests of the day for successful recreation programs for large and small groups of men and girls, in which round dancing has no part. There is also a chapter of games especially adapted to groups of girls. The material is not original: it is rather in the nature of a compilation gathered during several years of experimental recreation. Wherever possible due acknowledgment has been made, but in most cases the source is unknown.

Thanks are especially extended to the members of the 1913 and 1917 classes of the National Training School, and to the guests and counselors at Camp Altamont, N. Y., in the summer of 1917, for the very real service they have rendered in compiling suggestions here incorporated, all of which have been tested and found good.

EDNA GEISTER.

CONTENTS

ICE-BREAKERS

Games and Stunts
for
Large and Small Groups

ICE BREAKERS

CHAPTER I

ICE BREAKERS

The Receiving Line

IN order that every member of a large group may meet all other guests, use the continuous receiving line. The chaperons stand together; the men form one column, the girls another. The first man introduces himself to the first chaperon, is passed down the line, and then stands at the side of the last chaperon as a part of the receiving line. The first girl goes through the same procedure, then a man, a girl, and so on, each one standing in position as a part of the line, in turn, until the last one has passed down the line. This is especially good for a group of strangers, but there is a certain dignity and formality about it that makes it good for any kind of community group. It may be made decidedly humorous by the following addition: Each person on entering the room receives a slip of paper bearing directions to govern his hand-shaking in the receiving line. The "down-easter" grasps a hand and works it like a pump-handle; the "Frenchman" continuously bows with his hand on his heart; the Chinaman shakes his own hand complacently; and the débutante languidly extends two fingers,

1

or offers her hand on a level with her shoulder and gives one frigid shake. Others give the old time pressure which makes the tears start with its force as well as its fervor.

The Labyrinth

Guests stand in single file, first a man, then a girl, a man, a girl, etc., the director and chaperons leading. Each one extends his right hand forward to the one next in front and the left hand back, grasping his neighbors' extended hands. All march forward, circling to left and winding up into a spiral. When wound as far as possible, leaving plenty of space, the director calls a halt, and she alone about-faces, the rest of them keeping their lines absolutely straight. The leader then begins her way out from the center of the spiral, with the entire line following, passing out in a reverse spiral. This is done in the following manner: The leader shakes hands with and introduces herself to the one who was directly back of her, whom we shall call number two, immediately passing on to number three, four, five, and so on to the end of the spiral. As soon as she has passed number two, he begins the same performance, shaking hands with number three, then four, etc. Number three then begins, and each one in turn goes through the same procedure, thus making it inevitable that every guest has met every other one and that they have all met the hostess and the chaperons.

Dimes

A splendid method of breaking the ice in a large group is to give out ten dimes, one each to ten people, preferably bashful ones, who are told to tell no one about the possession of the dime, but are to count silently the people who shake hands with them. The group is told that ten dimes are in the pockets of ten people and that the twenty-second person who shakes hands with the holder of the dime gets it. No one knowing who has a dime, everyone immediately makes it his business to shake hands with every other person in the room. Three or four minutes are allowed. At the end of that time the dime-holders are asked to step to the front and in turn announce the prize-winners.

The Inquisition

Use the Grand March to form a double circle, every man having a partner. The couples march around to music until a whistle blows, when the men about face, girls still marching forward. At a second whistle every man takes a new partner and stops to talk to her for a minute and a half. At the end of that time the director can call any couple to the center of the room and ask what they know about each other as to name, occupation, city, town and state they originally came from, mutual acquaintances and likes and dislikes. All then march forward, and this is repeated at very short intervals. If the group is very large, a smaller circle within the large one can be handled very easily.

Blind Animal

For speed in breaking the ice in a strange group, Blind Animal has no equal. As each guest arrives, his name is written in large letters and pinned on his back, and he is asked to let no one see it. When all the guests have arrived, they are given cards and pencils and are told to get the names of as many other people as possible but to let no one get theirs. There is only one rule—no one is allowed to stand with his back against anything. So while Mr. Smith is trying to find out who the pretty girl in pink is, he is conscious that a girl in white is most determined in her effort to find out his name. The prize is given to the person whose name appears on the cards the fewest number of times. At a party where all the guests know each other they are given names of animals instead, and the problem then is to find out what kind of animal Frank Jones is. If he were a rhinoceros, anyone who found it out would write on his own card "Frank Jones—Rhinoceros."

Conversation

Couples in a double circle, men inside. Subject for conversation is announced, and each couple must talk on that subject till whistle blows. To make sure they do talk on the announced subject, any couple may be called to center of circle to give its views on that subject. All couples then march around to music till leader calls "Men reverse." Men about face and march in other direction, girls continuing in same direction till leader calls "Take partners," and a new subject is announced. Subjects may include, "Is June first too early for a man to wear a straw hat, etc., etc."

Neighbors

Formation—single circle with one person in the center who has the privilege of pointing unexpectedly to anyone in the circle and asking her the name of either her right or left neighbor, or both. If she cannot answer before the one in the center counts ten, she must change places with this inquisitor and remain there until she catches some one who does not know the names of her neighbors. Neighbors must change constantly. This is done through the order "Fruit Basket," which is given repeatedly and which means that everyone must find a new set of neighbors. Any one found standing next to a former neighbor may be called to the center of the circle as punishment.

To Find Partners

Grand March

In large groups the easiest method is to have all the men line up on one side of the room and all the girls on the other. They counter march, leaders turning abruptly away from center of room, marching, both leaders close to their own lines, to opposite end of room, where leaders meet and come up with partners. If the men can line up in a separate room, not seeing the girls until they get into the main room, it adds greatly to the excitement. In this case, the leaders join the lines as close to the door as possible.

The Celebrities

Distribute cards on which have been written the names of public or humorous characters, with the names of their partners on corresponding cards. For instance, Pa Ticklepitcher searches until he has found Ma Ticklepitcher, and Mr. I. M. Smart, has no peace until he has found Mrs. I. M. Smart.

Observation

On entering the room each man is given a paper and pencil, and is introduced to a lady with whom he is to talk for five minutes. At the end of that time he is asked to go to another part of the room and to write a minute description of her appearance, her dress, etc., etc. After ten minutes the papers are collected. Later in the evening, when refreshments are served, these slips are distributed among the men, who are told to find the lady fitting the description they hold.

Stuntification

The men may be given pieces of paper which specify that they are to do some stunt, *i. e.*, jump up and down, crow, sing, go to sleep, or do an aesthetic dance. Each girl holds a slip telling her what stunt her partner will do. She claims him when she recognizes his stunt— if she does recognize it.

The Chance

To find partners in smaller groups, have the girls stand in turn with one foot sticking out from under a curtain. The men of course choose.

Blind Man's Buff

Another way is to play the old-fashioned game of Blind Man's Buff. The girls form a circle; each man is blind-folded in turn and placed in the center with a cane, and the one whom he touches with the cane is to be his partner.

Valentine Partners

For finding Valentine partners, pin a number of red paper hearts on a sheet stretched between folding doors. The name of each man present is written on a heart.

When the guests enter the room, each lady is given an arrow made of red paper which has a number on it. When all have arrived, the ladies, one by one, are blindfolded, and each one tries to pin her arrow on a heart on the sheet. Each girl must remember her number; and just before refreshments are served, each heart is taken off in turn together with the nearest arrow.

Refreshments

When one "takes a chance," he appreciates most sincerely what he finally does get in the way of food. All refreshments are concealed in impromptu booths. If, for example, there are to be four kinds, there may be five booths, the extra one for napkins, and each one numbered. A Grand March leads past these booths, and each guest knocks on any one he chooses. Its presiding officer gives him his portion of whatever is concealed. It may be a banana. Whatever it is, that is the first course, and he, still marching, eats it "on the run." The march is continuous and leads again past the booths where each one chooses his second course, and so on through the five courses. The refreshments are placed in the booths in reversed order. For example, a first booth may contain cocoa; a second, cakes; the third, salad; the fourth, napkins; and the fifth, sandwiches.

See also Poverty Party refreshments.

CHAPTER II

Grouping People for Stunts

IF one has a very large company and wishes to divide them, each separate group to give a stunt, they may be divided in one of the following ways, a placard showing each group where to stand:

1. According to month of birth.
2. According to birthplace.
3. Red-headed, light-headed, black-headed, brown-headed, etc.
4. According to profession, teachers, students, clerks, soldiers, etc.
5. According to height, long, short, indifferent.
6. According to avoirdupois, fat, lean, middling.

Upsetting Exercises

A take-off on a setting-up drill. The class and teacher are dressed in the most ridiculous manner. The following commands are given while soft sweet music is played.

1. "Class, fall in" (fall all over each other).
2. "Line up according to fight" (fight for place).
3. "Right dress" (button up coats, collars, etc.).
4. "Class undress" (unbutton and start to take off coats, collars, etc.).

8

5. "Forward march. On toes march. Backward march."

6. "Class, halt" (with several counts).

7. "Eye rolling with mouth open."

8. "Cheek puffing alternately."

9. "Nose twitching alternately sidewards and up-wards."

10. "Winking alternately."

11. "Class, face rest."

12. "Foot placing forward, alternately" (clasp foot with both hands and lift it forward).

13. "Grasp nose with right hand, and right ear with left hand. Change."

14. "Hop toad position" (take an incorrect prone falling position with head downward, and on second count fall flat with hands extended).

15. "Tongue stretching forward."

16. "Head scratching alternately, right. Change left."

17. "Class fall out."

Intersperse such remarks as, "Less attention and more noise."

Goop Stunt

A sweater is buttoned around the lower part of the body, not coming any higher than the waist. A stick or umbrella is put through the sleeves with gloves attached at each end. A pillow case which is tucked in at the waist is put over the head with arms held high, holding it there. Be sure of a very secure fastening for both sweater and pillow case at waist line. The goop when so dressed gives the appearance of possessing a very large head and short body. He comes in wobbling as though he were top-heavy and sings this song in the most plain'tive, forlorn, hopeless tone possible, to almost any or no tune:

Song

I with I wuth a little bird,
I'd fly to the top of a tree,
I'd thit and thing my thad little thong,
But I can't thtay here by mythelf.

Chorus

I can't thtay here by mythelf,
I can't thtay here by mythelf,
I'd thit and thing my thad little thong,
But I can't thtay here by mythelf.

I with a wuth a little fith,
I'd think to the bottom of the thea,
I'd thit and thing my thad little thong,
But I can't thtay here by mythelf.

Chorus repeated

Alath, how little do we know
How many hearths are thad.
I long to thoothe thome twoubled bweatht,
And make thome thad heart glad.

Chorus repeated

Variation of this is to have three or four girls dressed like goops come in and dance. Any folk dance is made ridiculously funny in this way.

Bride and Groom

One person does this, with one side of the body dressed like a man, the other side like a woman. This is very easily done by putting on the man's clothes first, pulling the hair straight over to one side and to that side of the head pinning a man's soft hat, which has one side pushed into the other. The shoe on that side must be most masculine. The woman's clothes can be drawn together so that only one-half shows. For example, one sleeve of her waist can be pushed right through the other sleeve. The impersonator carries on a most animated conversation as if between a bride and groom. If the groom is talking she turns the groom side to the audience and talks in a deep bass voice. If it is the bride, she whirls that side around and talks in a decidedly feminine voice. They make love to each other, quarrel, make up, and enact a complete romance.

Italian Grand Opera

Arrange a touching love scene, having much dramatic action and singing, using such words as Spaghetti, Tamale, Macaroni, Parchesi, San Francisco, Caruso, Amato, etc. A mock accompaniment may be played on a piano without striking any of the keys, but with all the flourishes of an impresario.

Peggy

A girl is concealed so that only her hands show. Over these, clasped together, is tied a handkerchief on which are drawn the features of a woman. Questions are then asked of Peggy which are solemnly answered by a nod or shake of the "head." These questions may include

hits at some of those present. The little finger can be
moved, giving the appearance of eating.

Ventriloquist

One person is introduced as a famous ventriloquist,
and four or five are dressed up as dummies. The ventriloquist carries on an animated conversation with the
dummies, pretending to perform a genuine ventriloquist
stunt, by visibly moving her lips and yet trying to conceal it when the sounds come from the dummies' mouths.
In reality, of course, the persons inside the dummy
figures are answering her, in most mechanical tones,
moving their lips in the stiffest, most unnatural fashion.
The fun lies in the mistakes that are made towards the
end of the performance. For instance, the ventriloquist
might stop moving her lips, and a dummy continues
to talk. At the end, when the ventriloquist is not looking, the dummy figures suddenly come to life and walk
to the front of the stage and bow profusely, as the ventriloquist bows. The latter makes her exit in confusion.

The dialogue should be humorous, quick and snappy.

The Doctor Magician

Setting—Doctor's office.

Characters—Doctor with large spoons, empty bottles,
etc., at hand. Short fat woman who wants to get tall
and slender. Tall, thin woman who wants to get short
and plump.

Fasten two stuffed heads with features marked and
with hats on, on the ends of umbrellas. Just below each
one, with a fur boa or some neck piece to fill the gap,
loosely drape a long kimono. Open one umbrella and

have a very tall girl hunch down inside it, appearing to be a very short, fat woman. She waddles in to the office with great difficulty, and with much puffing and wheezing asks to be made thin. The doctor looks at her in dismay, then seizes a bottle and a huge spoon and pretends to pour some medicine down her throat and tells her to stand still one minute, after which the medicine will have worked and he can complete his treatment. The other umbrella is kept closed and a short girl gets under the kimono, holding the umbrella high above her head. She walks into the office with a fussy, nervous step and demands in a squeaky voice that she be made fat. The doctor stands on a chair and administers the same treatment. He then takes a squirt gun, and, filling it with an imaginary preparation, shoots it into the mouth of each, at which treatment the fat one's avoirdupois collapses and she shoots up in height, while the thin one rapidly spreads but sinks until she is short and fat. The short fat woman of course has closed her umbrella and stands up straight holding it high above her, while the tall thin woman opens her umbrella and pulls it way down. They descend upon the doctor and after embracing him depart in great joy. The conversation is impromptu.

Crazyola Victrola

The equipment is a large square box, with the open side facing a rear room. Only the top and the front of the box are visible to the audience, everything else being curtained off. On the top is a clothes wringer, in which are inserted the records, narrow slips of paper, yards in length. There is a hole in the front of the box in which a megaphone is placed. Before each feat an announcer puts his head in the box and in a nasal tone drawls out the subjects of the records. The scraping sound of graphophones is made by rubbing something rough against a tin can. As each "record" is put on, the paper is inserted, the crank is turned, the announcement is made and then the performers, who are in the room behind the curtain, stick their heads in their turn into the box and sing or speak through the megaphone.

The selections may be either good or very funny music, solos, duets and even quartets, or readings, the humorous ones being the most fitting.

Advertising

Different advertisements are acted out, to be guessed by the audience after all action has ceased. For example, "Colgate's lies flat on the brush" is illustrated by a girl placing a brush on the floor and lying flat on it; "Wool Soap" by a fat girl mournfully looking at her sweater which is four sizes too small since it was washed, etc.

Ford Stunt

The Bachelor Brother invites two Spinster Sisters to ride in his new Ford. The Ford is made of armchairs for automobile seats, an inverted folding chair for the engine with a lantern on it, and a handle attached, such as an ice cream freezer handle. Some one whirling an egg-beater behind the scenes, produces an exact Ford sound. The tourists dress up in ridiculous motoring clothes and with much ado and nervous shrill conversation get in, Bachelor Brother receiving minute directions as to how to drive. They remark on the beautiful scenery they pass, are arrested for speeding, run over a chicken (farmer produces feathers as evidence), have a blow-out, have nervous chills, one faints, and the Bachelor Brother works up quite a temper. The ride ends when the machine falls over an embankment.

Romeo and Juliet

Juliet stands on a ladder, dressed in white. Romeo, in plumed hat, velvet cloak, etc., stands below her, looking up, and the following dialogue takes place:

ROMEO—"It vas her, Oh, it vas mein luf. She schpeaks somedings aber I don't fershtand vat she say. Oh, see, she has her scheek on her handt. Oh, if that mitten on her handt vas me dot I might touch dat scheek!"

JULIET—"Ah, me!"

ROMEO—"Oh, schpeak, von dimes more, pright angel pird!"

JULIET—"Romeo, Romeo, ver you vas?"

ROMEO—"I took dhee at dhy vord und came.
    Call me, luf, und I come quick!"

JULIET—"How you got dot garten in?"

ROMEO—"Mit luf's light vings I der vall schump over like a geese pird."

JULIET—"If mein fader see you, it was petter if you diedt before you vas porn."

ROMEO—"I haf me one night's cloak to hide me in, und if you luf me it vas petter if I gone dedt here before dose pright eyes as some places oderwhere, ain't it?"

JULIET—"O Romeo, you make me plush aber you gant see dot in de night. O dost dhou luf me?"

ROMEO—"Schweed goil, I schwear by dot moon I luf dhee."

JULIET—"Oh, schwear not by dot moon. Sometimes he don't shine and such luf like dose I don't want."

ROMEO—"Dan vat I schall schwear py, fair geese pird?"

JULIET—"Don't schwear at all, but if dhou moost schwear, schwear py your own gracious self."

ROMEO—"So help me, gracious, I luf dhee."

JULIET—"Goot nightd, good nightd, I must me on der ped go."

ROMEO—"O golly, you gone away?"

JULIET "Vat goot for me gan you tonight hafe?"

ROMEO—"Dot you can gif me yourself und all your luf."

JULIET—"You got my luf pefore you ask him, and I gif him to you again und again, und again I must to ped now go. Goot nightd, goot nightd, goot nightd!"

ROMEO—"Der teufel! She vas gone! Oh, you agin pack? I got me skeerd, I dought you don't get agin pack."

JULIET—"Romeo, hist!"

ROMEO—"Schweed vone, I hist, I don'd gare if I hist the nightd through so you pin der hister. It vas so schweed to stand here."

JULIET—"It vas near morning und I vould haff dhee gone. I must on der ped go. I see dhee agin."

ROMEO—"Oh, me, Oh, me, dot vas too pad. Schleep, schweed schleep. I come me some odder nightd. Goot nightd, goot nightd."

The Mock Trial

Any subject may be used for the trial, but the more apt the charge, the better. Use well known people as witnesses, plaintiff, defendant, jury, etc. Much depends on securing capable "lawyers." Everything, while bearing an air of the greatest seriousness, should be made absolutely ridiculous in its application. Previous rehearsal spoils the fun.

A Mock Political Convention

This needs just a little bit of preparation and parts are assigned a few days ahead of time. The make-ups of well-known presidential candidates, the chairman of the convention, the policemen, the telegraph messenger boy can be well caricatured. A most dignified procession into the convention hall opens the events of the evening. A brief business meeting follows, and then the names of the respective candidates are placed in nomination. Personal allusions bring out sharp retorts and the speeches of the candidates themselves can give a spicy lesson in current events. Hurrying messenger boys and the ejection of some disqualified delegates lend diversion and interrupt the serious addresses.

Pipe Organ

Girls in black waists stand behind a curtain which comes up to the waist line.

Make pipes of heavy wrapping paper, large enough to go down over the girls' heads. These may be gilded. Slits may be made in each pipe over the girl's mouth. Any number of girls may be used, but five is sufficient, arranged with the tallest in the center. The girls hold out their hands stiffly with the fingers together, palms upward, for the keyboard. The organist sits on a stool and plays, making different movements as if some fingers were stops, etc. The girls make different sounds as they are played upon. A soloist may sing a touching song to the music. One pipe out of tune is very funny.

"Well, I Will"

One person gives this, twisting her mouth according to directions for each character. As she speaks for Sall, for instance, who calls Ma, she must twist her mouth like Sall's. At the end when she says for John, "What a blessing," etc., she must twist her mouth rapidly, to imitate the peculiar twists of each mouth.

"Ma's got a mouth like this" (lips pulled in).

"Pa's got a mouth like this" (lips parted and held stiffly apart like the mouth of a fish).

"Sall's got a mouth like this" (mouth twisted to left side).

"Sam, he's Sall's beau, he's got a mouth like this" (mouth twisted to right side).

"John went off to college and he's got a mouth like this" (mouth straight).

"One night Sam came to see Sall, and Sam said, 'Sall, will you marry me?' Sall said, 'I guess so.' 'Well, I wish you would.' 'Well, I will.'

"So that night they got married, and Sam had to blow out the candle" (blow). 'Sall, I can't blow this candle out, come see if you can.' 'All right.' 'Well, I wish you would.' 'Well, I will.' (Sall tries).

" 'Sam, I can't blow this candle out, I'll call Ma.' 'Well, I wish you would.' 'Well, I will. Ma, Ma! I wish you'd come and see if you can blow this candle out. Sam tried and I tried, and we can't blow it out so come and see if you can.' 'All right.' 'Well, I wish you would.' 'Well, I will.' (Tries blowing.) 'Sall, Sall, I can't blow this candle out, I'll call Pa.' 'Well, I wish you would.' 'Well, I will. Pa, Pa, come and see if you can blow this candle out, Sam tried and Sall tried and I tried and we can't blow it out. Come see if you can.' 'All right.' 'Well, I wish you would.' 'Well, I will.' 'Ma, Ma, I can't blow this candle out, I'll call John.' 'Well, I wish you would.' 'Well, I will. John, John, come and see if you can blow this candle out. Sam tried, Sall tried, Ma tried and I tried and we can't blow it out. Come and see if you can.' 'All right.' 'Well, I wish you would.' 'Well, I will.' '' (Blows it out.) ''What a blessing it is to have one straight mouth in the family.''

Have You 'Eared about Hairy?

The one who tells the news does so slowly, but melodramatically, slapping the second man on the part of the body named in his story. ''Chester'' merely listens with mouth wide open, jumping nervously at each slap, but at the end knocking down the first man. The two come in from opposite sides and bump into one another. The first one immediately becomes excited and says, ''Hello, Chester (chest). Have you eared (ear) about Hairy? (hair). He jest (chest) got back (back) from the front (knees) to do feats (stepping on both feet) for the army (arm). Hip hip (hips) hooray for the army!'' (arms), whereupon Chester knocks him flat.

Three Land-Lubbers in Bathing

Three people enter, dressed in bathing costumes. They approach imaginary water, put in the tips of their toes, draw back, feel the water with their hands, shiver, put water on their necks, venture in, draw feet up high, take hold of hands, advance and finally all duck down and at that moment all give a sudden yell, turn about and dash off the stage. As all has been absolutely still up to the yell, it is a surprise.

The Coquette

Cast—the coquette, a maid, four gentlemen callers.
Scene—a sitting room.

The coquette, dressed in a very fancy gown, sits reading, when a ring is heard. The maid, with a large tray, goes to the door, and, after taking in the card, ushers in the first suitor. He presents the girl with a bunch of artificial flowers, after which they sit down and carry on a very animated pantomime conversation. Soon another ring is heard, and the maid again goes to the door. She brings in the card of second suitor. The coquette, embarrassed and excited, snatches her first caller from his chair, forces him to his knees, and makes him hold the maid's tray over his head. She grabs up a table cover and throws it over the tray, thus covering the man's head, and converting him into a table. The second suitor is then ushered in. He brings a box of candy, and after presenting it, another pantomime conversation is held. A third caller arrives with a gift, and while he is being met at the door by the maid, the unfortunate second is converted into a hatrack by covering his head with an overcoat and thrusting his arms part way through the sleeves and hanging a hat upon one of his arms. Caller Number Three comes in leisurely, puts his hat on the rack, takes off his gloves, and after he has made love to Miss Jones for a few minutes the doorbell again rings. Caller Number Four is announced but after a moment's reflection, Miss Jones now conceives the idea of making Caller Number Three into an armchair; he is accordingly put down on a chair, and a cover is thrown over him to make him resemble an armchair. Caller Number Four comes in and sits down in the armchair which hits the hatrack. The hatrack in turn top-

ples over the table so they all go in a heap on the floor.
The screen is quickly turned or drawn.

Alphabetical Romance

S. O. S. B. V. D.
Q. E. D. X. Y. Z. P. D. Q.

A girl sits in an imaginary garden with some one
holding branches of trees, etc., over her head. A lover
comes in. She is greatly surprised, cries, "B. V. D."
and falls into his arms, whereupon he says feelingly,
"S. O. S.!" The romance continues, they are absorbed
in each other, he brings forth a box of candy, finally
they quarrel and at last make up. All this is shown
through facial expression, gesticulations and by using
such combinations of letters as shown above. The romance can be enlarged upon as desired.

The Dwarf Exhibit

Two persons play the dwarf, a third acting as an
exhibitor who should prepare beforehand a humorous
speech setting forth history and accomplishments of
the dwarf. By an improvised screen hide all the prepa-
rations in dressing the dwarf.

To arrange and dress the dwarf, place a table on the
platform and cover it with a cloth or curtain that will
reach to the floor. One person stands behind the table
and places his hands on it; these with his arms form
the feet and legs of the dwarf. Over his arms should be
drawn a pair of boy's trousers and on his hands should
be a pair of shoes. The trousers should be drawn down
until they reach the heels like a man's. A second person
stands behind the first and passes his arms under the
first one's shoulders. By putting a coat over the arms

and buttoning it down the figure of the first person and then throwing a cape around his neck, so arranged as to cover the head of the person behind, the dwarf's dress is completed. The hands of the second person act as the hands of the dwarf, and as the latter makes his appearance, they raise his hat when he bows to the audience. The exhibitor should then recite the various accomplishments of the dwarf, including dancing and even his ability to suspend himself in the air without support. The dwarf should then be invited to entertain the audience, and he should begin by making a little speech in either a thin falsetto or a heavy bass voice, or by speaking any humorous piece. The second player makes gestures to the speech which in themselves will create a laugh. Then the dwarf begins to dance. The hands of the first performer do this, and all of a sudden in the midst of a quick step they are both lifted from the table and remain suspended in the air for a quarter of a minute. Then they drop to the table again and the dwarf appears to be exhausted with the unusual effort.

In making his parting salute to the audience the dwarf astonishes them all by putting both feet to his mouth and throwing kisses with his toes.

The Hawaiian Musicians

Several girls wear black jerseys and skirts made of hay. They stand together in a little group on the stage and in a ridiculous fashion burlesque Hawaiian singing. They sing any foolish song, dragging out the notes in long, lingering tones or shrilly, in true Hawaiian fashion.

One tune used successfully is, ''One grasshopper

jumped right over the other grasshopper's back," etc.,
to the tune of "John Brown's Body."

Tight Rope Walker

Stretch a large, thick rope across the floor and have
the performer walk back and forth on it, going through
the various antics of a real tight rope walker. She may
be dressed in any funny costume, and should wear the
usual kimono over it, struggling to retain her balance
by means of a tiny parasol. First, after much hard
work, she may remove her kimono and then carry on
her other various tight rope walking acts, for example,
balancing a pencil or similar object on her nose or chin
by having a piece of chewing-gum stuck on the end of
the object and sticking it in place. The performer must
know the usual stunts of a tight rope walker and it is
very amusing to see them carried out on the floor instead of in mid-air. She closes the performance by falling off the rope in realistic fashion.

The Champion High Singers

Three or four people enter, and crouching down on
their heels, sing a song in a very low key. They rise
gradually, stand straight, then on tiptoe, and finally
climb on chairs, raising the key of the song with each
process until they are singing at impossible heights.

The Inverted Quartet

A quartet, with only their heads showing above a
sheet, sing a really beautiful song. At the end of their
song they apparently stand on their heads and repeat
the chorus, only their feet showing. This is done by

having them put socks and shoes on their hands and raising them up above the sheet when heads are ducked. Just before the end, one of the people who holds the sheet accidentally drops his end.

The Cat Fight

Two people enter dressed in black cat costumes, and do the Oxdansen from "Folk Dances and Singing Games" by Elizabeth Burchenal.

Pig Tail Quartet

Four girls who have good voices and long braids stand in a row with their backs to the audience. The music-master produces a most wonderful quartet by pulling on the braids as he would pull bell-ropes. After a good selection, they may sing a funny one, striking wrong notes, etc., and at the end the director by mistake, pulls off a false pig tail.

Impersonations

Famous and local characters are impersonated, both in appearance, action and talk, the audience guessing who is being impersonated. No guesses are allowed until the character has finished his performance.

The Doll Shop

A fastidious buyer and her bored young daughter come into a doll shop to search for a doll, "Something different, don't you know!" The shop keeper calls out his dolls one by one. They come in mechanically, perform the stunts he calls on them to do and line up glassy-eyed against the wall, where startling things may happen, such as one throwing a stiff fit because a wrong wire has been touched. Personal hits at those taking the part of dolls may be made. The buyers leave soon with such remarks as, "The dolls have no life—no animation —so common, don't you know!"

Misspelled Spelling

The following pieces are made ridiculously funny by exchanging the first letters of words:

I.   Once a big molice pan
    Met a bittle lum
    Sitting on a sturb cone
    Chewing gubber rum.
    "Hi," said the molice pan,
    "Won't you simmie gum?"
    "Tixxy on your nin type,"
    Said the bittle lum.

II.   Heard about my little dog difo?
    Bought him when he pas a wup,
    Taught him to stand on his lind hegs,
    And hold his lont fregs up.

III.   The night was stark and dormy, the wind went
      beeping swy,
    The lightning fashed in flury and the runder
      thored on high,
    A little old cog labin stood by a rountain moad
    And from its woken brindow a flickering shandle
      code,
    A faint but biendly freakon it wone upon the shay

To those githout its widence who might go star
afray.
The dabin core stood open and from it meared a
pade
Intent on sowing gumware and in rad glags ar-
rayed,
And when she law the sightning, and heard the
rashing dain
She wumbled to the tether and dut the shore
again.

A Chinese Movie

Run a movie film backwards.

Redroad Lyceum Bureau

A Lyceum Bureau is represented. Applicants are
received and tested, each one being asked to give a sam-
ple of his art. This may be the means of getting over
a really delightful program interspersed with much
nonsense. Several of the applicants are rejected for
various reasons: one because of the size of her ears;
and another because his nose wiggles when he sings.

Ten-in-One Medicine

The reception room to a doctor's office is represented,
and a screened corner near the front of the stage serves
as the private office. No properties needed, but a large
bottle of medicine. Patients fill the reception room
while awaiting the doctor's arrival. Their mutual sus-
picion and scorn for each other's probable ailments
makes the waiting interesting. When the doctor arrives,
there is a bedlam as to who came first. A very stout

lady and her extremely thin daughter win out. The mother is much concerned as to the lack of size of her daughter. The doctor feels her pulse, thumps her back, makes her sing "Ah," and gives her a large dose of medicine, asking the mother to bring her back in the morning. The next patient is a decided business woman who has a bunion. He feels her pulse, thumps her back, makes her sing "Ah," and gives her a large dose of his one medicine, and asks her to call again the next day. The same treatment is given every patient: the little boy whose mother thought he was too fat; the girl who wished to become beautiful; the man bent forward with rheumatism, etc., etc. The curtain drops for a minute, and the time changes to the next morning in the same office. Furious indignation is registered because of the radical effect of the medicine. The thin girl has become positively huge (with the aid of pillows and by bulging out the cheeks). The lady suffering with a bunion comes in on crutches; the man who was bent forward with rheumatism bends way back in the other direction, and so forth. Each one registers his complaint in the most furious way, and it ends by their surrounding the doctor and forcing him to drink the entire contents of the bottle. While he is surrounded by them and hidden from the audience, a bald wig may be clapped on his head, and a huge pasteboard nose attached. The scene ends with the patients hooting in derision at the doctor, who totters off the stage.

The Penny Arcade

People act as the machines. Each one has a box on one hand with a slot in it for the penny. Any sort of rubber hosing does for the tube which runs from the mouth of the machine to the ear of the listener. When a penny is dropped in, the machine starts sometimes with a funny song and again with a monologue on the listener, in a cracked voice.

The Baby Show

Well-known adults dressed for the part, with mothers in attendance. They perform the usual tricks of babies showing off for company.

The Victrola

The group is invited to assist in making a Victrola record. This is done in a *bona fide* way, and this record is then played. Someone asks to have it played again, and a blank record is put on instead, while a person who is concealed gives a monologue in a nasal tone, getting in several hits on people in the party.

Impromptu Artists

Four or five people are chosen to be artists, and they stand facing the audience. Large paper bags are put over their heads. They are given pieces of charcoal and told to make features on the front of their bags, eyes. eyebrows, ears, nose and mouth. The mouth must be smiling!

Bedlam

A popular song is sung in English. It is sung then in turn in Swedish, Norwegian, Hebrew, French, Hawaiian, and Italian by people dressed in costume. Finally all come out and sing the song together, each in her own tongue.

State Parade

An effective out-of-door or large room stunt which needs very little preparation is the State Parade. When everyone has arrived, the entire group is divided according to the state each one came from originally—all Iowans in one group, Kansans in another, etc. It is a wise plan to see that there is a good leader in each group, even if one has to be grafted on! Each group then prepares, with impromptu costumes and properties, some characteristic state stunt or float for the parade. No names are attached, and the parade passes by the judges' stand, all through the grounds or rooms and back to the judges' stand where the decisions for the funniest and most characteristic stunts are given. As an example, Illinois, being the Sucker State, could be represented by "babies" howling lustily and intermittently absorbing milk from huge bottles seated in wagons disguised as baby buggies and attended by fierce nurses.

The Rejuvenation

Equipment—a huge grinding machine which has for its entrance a stile effect, one stairway leading up and one going down into the internals. There should be two exits, the one opening on the stage, and the other covered and opening behind the scenes. There is a large crank on the stage side which is turned each time a victim is taken into the machine, with a machine-like sound accompanying. The audience is told a fanciful tale about the famous rejuvenating doctor being in town just one night; how several people had put in their applications early, and were about to take the treatment. First might come a decidedly tall thin girl who wanted to become an aesthetic dancer. She demonstrates her desire in a most awkward way, for the Doctor cannot understand English. She is then started up the stairs to the machine. The Doctor manipulates certain valves, and the operation is on. Almost immediately appears a short compact girl, who does a beautiful aesthetic dance. The next applicant may be an old, old lady who wishes to acquire the talent of whistling. Her rejuvenation takes the form of a person who is the finest whistler obtainable. A dignified professor may wish to learn to clog dance. He does. So the entire program may be given some of it only humorous, but with a great deal of it made up of real talent.

Shadow Pictures

Stretch a sheet to fill the space in a doorway. If the sheet is evenly wet, the shadows are much clearer. The room in which the audience is seated is dark. A lamp is placed about six feet behind the center of the sheet in the other room. All actors play their parts between the light and the sheet, as close to the sheet as possible.

One suggestion for shadow pictures is to act poems in pantomime as the words are read aloud. Only verses with action are used, and the action burlesqued. Well-known characters in nursery rhymes like "Little Boy Blue," "Little Bo-Peep," "Red Riding Hood," "Old King Cole," etc., as well as some of the guests present, may be shown on the curtain and guessed by the audience.

A dentist may be shown pulling a tooth. A young lady may be shown sitting at a small table and about to dine. She raises the cover of a large soup toureen, and out jumps a live kitten. A teacher applying the birch to a squirming youngster, or a grandmother making vigorous use of soap and scrubbing brush to a small grandson are good subjects. Use the old operation stunt with various tools made of cardboard. Pour an anaesthetic into the victim by placing a megaphone or large funnel in line with his mouth and leading into a bucket below. Bucket after bucket of water can be poured in this way. Failing in this, have a block of wood alongside the victim's head on the table, and use a good size mallet on the block. The shadows, of course, make it appear as if you were hitting the victim on the forehead each time. The operation can then proceed, and your own ingenuity will suggest the various articles that can be removed from his interior and later put in again. By loosening the hair and letting it fall over the face, a girl may appear like a man with a beard; bending the finger over the nose gives one a very queer looking hooked nose in the shadow and entirely alters the appearance of the face. Covering oneself up in a sheet and then extending the arms gives one the appearance of a large bat.

Events may be numbered if guests' shadows are to be thrown upon sheet, and a guessing contest made out of Shadow Pictures.

Pantomime

The stunts following are acted out in pantomime, accompanied by a most dramatic reading of the story.

"Lord Ullin's Daughter"

The poem, by Thomas Campbell, may be found in most of the older collections of poems or ballads.

Suggestions for staging—A sheet, with a person at

each corner to keep it waving, represents the sea; a clothes-basket serves as a boat, and tennis racquets as the oars.

Cast—Boatman, lovers, father, horsemen.

The Eskimo Tragedy

Suggestions for staging—Footlights, several red-headed girls with paper bags on heads labeled, "Ye footlights," bags to be removed when play begins. Chairs draped with sheets, labeled, "Ye Icebergs." A tall girl at either side of the stage labeled, "Ye Curtain Pole." Two or three girls with frills of colored paper around their necks and frilled paper caps are brought in by the stage manager and seated behind the footlights, around each is fastened a band of red paper, to represent a flower pot, and each is labeled "Ye Potted Plant."

Cast—Eskimo, Eskimaid, Fido, the Dog, Eskimurderer, the Rival.

Costumes—Eskimo and Eskimaid in fur coats and with fur muffs on the head and on each leg. Fido is represented by a girl, on all fours, covered with a fur rug. On the rug is the sign "Fido." Eskimurderer is dressed much as the Eskimo.

Properties—Fur collars, muffs, etc., to line the grave. Moth balls. Large spice or pepper box.

> Mid Greenland's polar ice and snow
> Where watermelons seldom grow—
> It's far too cold up there, you know—
> There lived a bold young Eskimo.
>
> Beneath the selfsame iceberg's shade,
> In fur of bear and seal arrayed—

Not over cleanly, I'm afraid,
There lived a charming Eskimaid.

Throughout the six-months night they'd spoon—
O, ye in love, think what a boon!
To stop at ten is far too soon
Beneath the silvery Eskimoon.

The hated rival now we see,
You spy the coming tragedy—
But I can't help it, don't blame me—
An Eskimucker vile was he.

He spied the fond pair there alone,
He killed them with his axibone.
You see how fierce the tale has grown—
The fond pair died with an Eskimoan.

Two graves were dug deep in the ice
And lined with fur, moth-balls, and spice.
The two were buried in a trice,
Quite safe from all the Eskimice.

Now Fido comes. Alas, too late—
I hope it's not indelicate
These little incidents to state—
The Eskimurderer he ate.

Upon an Eskimo to sup
Was too much for an Eskipup.
He died. His Eskimemory
Is thus kept green in verse by me.

The Umha Family

1.—Mr. Umha enters dressed as an old farmer.

2.—Mrs. Umha, big and fat, enters dressed like a farmer's wife.

3.—A girl enters on all fours, dressed as a mule, drawing a large cardboard box with no bottom, for a sleigh. Wears a sweater with hay sticking through.

4.—Children enter one by one dressed in ridiculous costumes, and take their places in the sleigh.

5.—The mule slips and slides, and finally falls down, the sleigh upsets and they all fall out.

6.—Several doctors and nurses rush in and bind up the wounds of the injured children.

7.—They then bury the mule.

8.—All jump out and shout Um ha ha.

Come and listen to me and you shall hear
A story of old, most wondrous queer
Of a family known both far and near
By the funny name of Umha-ha.

1.—Mr. Umha said one day
He thought he'd take the family sleigh
And ride upon the frozen snow,

2.—And Mistress Umha said she'd go.
They took the family, of course,
Including, too, the family horse.

3.—He was a mule, and a big one too,
You could see his ribs where the hay stuck through.

4.—There was Tim and Duley Umhaha.
Rose and Julie Umhaha,
Lizzie Minnie Umhaha,

Big fat Jennie Umhaha,
Fourteen people in one sleigh,
They started out to spend the day.
But luck will have it as it will;
When they struck the top of the hill
The hill was slippery and down they flew.
How fast they went they never knew.
The time they made it can't be beat,
And the old mule had no use for its feet.
He looked like a bird or a ship in sail
And he flew with his ears and steered with his tail.
'Twas a mile to the bottom and the bottom was mud
5.—And they all struck the bottom with a sickening thud.
And Tim and Duley they were dazed,
Rose and Julie they were crazed,
Lizzie Minnie bumped her nose
Big fat Jennie she was froze.
6.—Fourteen doctors came from town
7.—And they buried the mule down under the ground
('Cause you never see a dead mule lying around).
It took four days to haul them home,
And when they found they'd broken no bones
They all jumped up and thanked their stars,
8.—And they all cried Umha-ha-ha-ha.

Wild Nell

The following tale is acted in pantomime, as if in the form of moving pictures:

"Ladies, gentlemen and others: We take great pleasure in presenting to you to-night the —————— Film

Company, Limited, very limited, in a moving burlesque entitled, 'Wild Nell, the Pet of the Plains,' or 'Her Final Sacrifice.' May I introduce Lady Vere de Vere, the English heiress, Handsome Harry, the King of the Cow Boys, Sitting Bull, the Indian Chief, Bull Durham, his Accomplice, Hula Hula, the Medicine Woman, and Wild Nell, the Pet of the Plains.''

As the names are read the characters come in from the right for an introductory bow and pose in character as on a movie screen. Lady Vere de Vere, in burlesque evening dress, flutters to the center, curtsies and exits left. Handsome Harry, in cow-boy's costume, wooden pistol, sombrero, with great strides and swing of arms, faces front, tips his hat in three directions, and strides off. Sitting Bull, in blanket-shawl, paint and head-dress of feathers waddles in looking at the audience with a fierce frown. Bull Durham imitates him. Hula Hula in squaw costume, smoking a pipe, is indifferent to every one. Wild Nell, in western costume, hands on hips and with a ''come-get-me'' wink, flits across the stage. (Wild Nell should be small and very vivacious.)

While the story is being read, the characters cross back, acting their lines. ''Lady Vere de Vere leaves her ancestral home for America.'' (Crosses stage backwards, throwing kisses toward wings, and bumps Handsome Harry, who is watching her with great interest; registers surprise.) Handsome Harry lifts hat, suggests walk, offers arm and pair leave in direction Lady Vere de Vere was going, to left. ''Wild Nell sees the meeting and her soul trembles with jealousy.'' (Nell enters, registers wild jealousy, shows great emotion and goes back to wing.) ''Sitting Bull and his accomplice plan to capture the English heiress.' (Bull tiptoes stiffly to

center and beckons Durham, who imitates him exactly.
They plot, scanning the horizon in unison. This is
done in the following manner: they meet in the center
front, go to opposite corners, look all about and come
back to confer in center front. Next, go to back corners
of stage in same manner, conferring again in center
front.) "They hide behind a prairie-dog hut." (They
take four steps in unison to right and squat together.)
"Lady Vere de Vere strolls across the plains." (She
zigzags over the stage, very elaborately breaking off
flowers, reaching anywhere, occasionally smelling the
bunch. She even goes so far as to pick one from Sitting Bull's head, blandly ignoring their presence.) "She
sits upon a cactus bush to rest." (Assumes sitting
posture beside the Indians, two steps away from her.)
"The Indians seize her." (They creep up to either
side of Lady Vere de Vere, grabbing her with much
gusto. Lady Vere de Vere registers yelling. Indians
swing her backward and forward as though wrestling.)
"They seat her upon their horse and carry her away."
(Lady Vere de Vere is between Indians. The three
together step back once, left side once, take high step
as though mounting, turn half right as they do so and
gallop off, Bull Durham pulling the reins, Lady Vere
de Vere screaming, Sitting Bull slapping an imaginary
horse.) "Wild Nell sees the capture, and her heart is
torn 'twixt love and duty." (Enters from left, looking
after departing Indians, alternates pleasure and worry.)
"Duty prevails and she calls Handsome Harry. She
tells the harrowing tale and they start in pursuit."
(Harry enters on horseback. He stops the horse and acts
dismounting, listens to Nell, motions her up behind.
They mount and gallop off. Height contrast wanted

here.) "The Indians gain." (Indians and Lady Vere de
Vere gallop across stage right to left.) "Harry and Wild
Nell follow. The redskins' horse grows tired." (Gallop
across right to left as before but slower.) "The white
men gain." (Before they get to the middle of the stage,
shout the next line, which they execute exactly in the
middle.) "But their horse goes lame." (Both hop heavily
on right foot, dragging left.) "Indians go up the river
in a canoe." (Indians paddle slowly together.) Lady
Vere de Vere puts hands up to mouth and screams.
Walks in middle as though seated in the middle of a
canoe.) "The brave rescuers discover another canoe
and continue the pursuit." (Harry in front taking
long dignified strokes, Nell behind making short wild
dashes. As they approach the center.) "They strike
a snag." (On Harry's next down stroke on the side
of the audience, Nell goes over the side. Three short
jabs, one long one and then as calm and dignified as
before.) "The Indian Medicine Woman sits at her
camp fire waiting for her braves to bring home the
bacon." (Hula Hula comes in and squats in the center.
Acts building fire and warming hands, pipe in mouth.)
"The braves bring in their captive and the Indian
woman decrees her death." (Squaw looks Lady Vere
de Vere over and then executes thumbs down or similar
sign.) "They tie her to a stake and commence an Indian war dance." (Squaw starts a fire. Sitting Bull
leads dance, squaw in middle, three short circles about
Lady Vere de Vere. During the second circle Handsome
Harry and Nell arrive at the edge of the screen and
watch. In the middle of the third, Harry starts winding lasso over head. Indians keep bunched.) "The
rescuers arrive in the nick of time and with one throw

of the lasso, cowboy captures savages." (They fall together.) "One bullet does for them all." (Harry
lowers the pistol or just his finger, indicating shot by
jerk or kick. The three Indians drop together on their
knees.) "Wild Nell unites the lovers." (The lovers
embrace.) "Her duty done, the favorite of the fron-
tiersmen makes her final sacrifice." (While the lovers
embrace, Nell, in center of stage, takes knife from girdle
and in great deliberation stabs herself and falls straight
back with a thud. Harry jumps to her side, feels for
her heart beat, rises, slowly shakes his head, and removes
his hat.)

Suitable moving picture music adds a great deal to
the effect. Make a great deal of every point, Wild Nell,
for instance, going into an ecstasy of emotion, tearing
her hair, etc., whenever she sees the lovers together.

Paul Revere

Paul Revere done in pantomime is very effective.

CHAPTER III

Family Party

As each guest arrives he is given a slip which assigns him to a family group. Each group may be made up of six or eight members, including perhaps Pa and Ma Ladderbean, the Ladderbean twins, the baby, and Europea Ladderbean. At a signal the members of families get together, each family is given a bundle made up of enough properties for that family, properties to include such articles as a pair of overalls, false mustache, wrapper, child's dress, neckties, and baby's bottle. Assign a certain place to each family and allow fifteen minutes for them to dress and arrange for some stunt for entertainment. Ma can make a little speech, baby can recite, the twins can sing and Pa can take off Ma getting ready to entertain the Ladies' Aid. A prize is given the family showing the finest artistic sense.

Basket Social

The old-fashioned basket social is always popular. Each girl brings a box of lunch, artistically wrapped, prepared for two people, and with nothing on the outside to show to whom it belongs, but with her name on a slip on the inside. The boxes are auctioned off and only when all have been sold are the men allowed to open them and find out the names of their partners.

Poverty Party

Evidence of most pitiful poverty should be shown in clothes, decorations and refreshments. For refreshments a salted peanut, a quarter of a sweet pickle and a cracker are served on small wooden plates. After these are eaten with no word of apology from the hostess for the scarcity of food, she announces one more game before going home. This begins with a Grand March and ends with *real* food.

Birthday Party

The birth month of each person may be ascertained upon his arrival, and groups formed for each month of the year. Each group is asked to represent its month by impromptu costume and stunt. The months may march in, headed by Father Time, but not arranged in their natural order. Father Time then calls upon each group, by number, for its stunt, and the guests determine which month is being represented. June may be represented by a restless schoolroom and then release; October by Hallowe'en pranks and the usual irate old man; April Fool by a child giving a wonderful cornet solo, which continues when he takes the cornet from his mouth; August by a camp-meeting; January by Father Time and a baby enacting a touching farewell scene; March by an electric fan blowing the actors out of the scene; May by Moving Day; November by stomach aches; December by children being painfully good. The prize is given to the group doing the most characteristic stunt.

Progressive Peanut

The idea is the same as for any progressive game, the winning couple moving up one table. A bowl of peanuts is on each table, with four hatpins supplied. In turn each one spears for peanuts, using a hatpin only. The couple getting the most peanuts moves up one.

Miscellaneous Progressive Party

The same idea as in progressive card games. Instead of cards, various contests are arranged for each table. Some of them may be as follows:

1. Flipping cards into a hat from a certain distance.
2. Tiddly Winks.
3. Jack Straws.
4. Fish Pond.
5. Spearing peas or peanuts.
6. Lifting beans with a lead pencil.
7. Making words out of one long word.

This list can be added to indefinitely, for any child's game can be made one of the events.

Backward Party

Invitations may be written backwards by means of a mirror. Guests are to come dressed backwards. Hair may be combed backwards, and the backward idea used in almost every detail of dress. Guests are to come up the back steps backwards, in through the back door; shake hands backwards, saying goodbye instead of greeting their friends. The first event of the evening is to sing "Good Night Ladies." Even games may be played backwards, and the entire evening program reversed. As to refreshments, after dinner mints and coffee may

be served first, reversing absolutely the usual schedule.
The salad may have the lettuce leaf on top, and the
napkin is passed at the end.

Baby Party

Grown-down children are invited, dressed in babies'
clothes, carrying milk bottles, rattles, etc. Baby games
are played; baby pictures enlarged on a screen, and
their owners guessed; and even baby refreshments served,
with sustaining food later!

Circus

The circus is always well received if given out of doors.
Very little screened-off space, such as a pavilion offers,
is necessary, almost all the events being easily adaptable
to out-of-door conditions. There are the usual clowns,
the flower and refreshment booths, venders of all kinds,
Hiram and Mirandy in from the country, a hobo band
to furnish music, the magic fish pond, the negro quar-
tette, officious policemen, trained elephants stepping on
everyone's toes, hit the dummy, side shows with fat
and thin ladies, human beings with bear feet, and of
course, the inevitable wild man from Borneo.

The program could further include:

1. Baby Show. See Index.
2. The Crazy House. Difficult passageways made with
   curtains and screens.
3. The Penny Arcade. See Index.
4. The Chamber of Horrors. A First-Aid dummy is
   most effective.
5. Ventriloquist. See Index.
6. Tight Rope Walker. See Index.

7. Character Photography. Take impression of face with piece of paper.

8. Fortune Telling. Any library has "Signs of the Zodiac." Have these copied on slips, and the appropriate month given to each customer.

9. Swimming Match. Posters showing a swimming pool with several swimmers racing. The show proves to be a match swimming in a saucer of water.

10. The Dwarf Exhibit. See Index.

11. The Quack Doctor. See Index.

12. Crazyola Victrola. See Index.

Hallowe'en Party

The hostess, wearing a mitten filled with cooked oatmeal, shakes each guest's hand.

If possible, have the door-knobs charged with electricity. It doesn't hurt and certainly causes unexpected movements.

Before a guest is allowed to enter the room in which the party is to be given, he must eat a long strip of cold, boiled macaroni.

Cat Game

Have the room partially darkened. As many people as possible sit around a sheet, holding it with their left hands. It is announced that the parts of a cat will be passed. No one is allowed to look under the sheet. Everything is passed in right hands. The names of the parts are called out as they are handed to the first person.

1. Head—a ball of yarn with hairpins stuck through.
2. The eyes—oysters.
3. The tail—any fur.
4. Claws—any claws from an old fur.
5. Inside—dough, well floured.
6. Teeth—false ones if possible, or beads.
7. Tongue—pickle.
8. Hide—a muff.

Suggested Games from Ice Breakers

1. Mystic Book
2. Scent Push
3. I See a Ghost
4. Awkward Eating Race
5. Cracker Relay
6. Standing High Jump
7. Blind Obstacle
8. Brother, I'm Bobbed

Unmasking

Unmasking may be made a game. March about the room masked, come to a stile (arrangement of table and chairs), cross it, unmask, all the dark-haired people going on one side, light-haired to the other, according to judges stationed there, and then follows a tug of war.

Contests

There may be contests for the fattest girl, the prettiest, the one who can make the worst face, etc.

Stunts

For stunts, see Shadow Pictures.

Fortunes

Apple Peeling

As to fortunes, there is the inevitable peeling an apple and throwing the peeling over the shoulder to see what initial it forms.

Pumpkin Fortune

Blindfold the victim, twirl her about three times, and have her spear at a pumpkin with a long hat pin previously placed in her hand. The alphabet may be cut upon the pumpkin, and the first three letters she strikes are the first letters of the name of her husband, his profession, and the adjective describing him.

Destiny

A girl's destiny may be settled according to which of three pans she puts her finger in when she is blindfolded. The pans are shifted so that she cannot tell their location.

1. Soapy water—Early widow.
2. Clear water—Happy marriage.
3. Empty dish—Independent spinster.

Signs of the Zodiac

Any library has "Signs of the Zodiac." Have these copied on slips, and the appropriate month given to each applicant.

Fortune Hunting

A ring, a piece of money, and a thimble are hidden in different places in the room where the guests are to be entertained. This game may be the first of the evening. The player who finds the ring will be married first and live happily ever after; the one who finds the money will have wealth; and the one who finds the thimble will live unmarried to the end of his or her life.

Fortune Gifts

The hostess collects a number of small articles, each suggestive of some profession or business; an army and navy button, a pen-point, a palette, a box of pills, etc. There should be as many articles as there are girls invited. They are wrapped in paper and placed in a large bag. Without being allowed to look inside, each girl chooses one and thereby settles her fate. The one who gets the palette for example, will marry a sign painter. A tray of sealed envelopes is handed about for the men. They contain pictures of girls; one a cook; another a dressmaker, an actress, a suffragette, etc.

[In addition, see Number Fortune and Maiden's Fortune.]

Palmistry

If one is willing to study up even a little on Handwritings, Palmistry, and Thumb Prints, one can always get splendid material at libraries, and the enjoyment it creates makes it more than worth while. To get good thumb-prints, have the subject dip her thumb in some water color and press it on white blotting paper.

As to refreshments, if possible plot out a long and devious course filled with obstacles which must be crossed in order to get any of the refreshments. When the goal is finally reached, let the prize be only the refreshments suggested for Poverty Party.

Popularity Parties

The following are two typical "recreation programs" with no round dancing, for groups varying from fifteen to two hundred, of girls only or of girls and men. It may be used as a foundation on which to build other programs.

An informal sing while the crowd is gathering has proved more effective than the informal game. The evening proper usually begins with the receiving line, into which everyone must go. Any of the mixing games in Ice Breakers may be used instead of the receiving line, or immediately following it. After that, the program may run somewhat as follows, although it is almost impossible to follow a plan exactly.

First evening:

1. Grand March — Figures 1, 2 and 4
2. Newspaper Race
3. We Won't Go Home
4. Going to Jerusalem
5. Folding Chair Relay
6. Animated Adjectives
7. Popularity
8. Suitcase Race
9. Living Alphabet
10. Rig-a-jig
11. Refreshments
12. General Singing— Song Contests
13. This is My Nose
14. Puppies Fly
15. Unknown Stunt
16. Merry-Go-Round
17. Virginia Reel
18. Good Night, Ladies

Second Evening:

1. Grand March — Figures 1, 2, 3, 4, 5
2. Blind Obstacle Race
3. Noriu Miego
4. Going to Jerusalem
5. Stunt—Wild Nell
6. Do This, Do That
7. Popularity

8. Magic Music
9. Cracker Relay
10. Nigarepolska
11. Refreshments
12. Singing
13. Puzzle Words
14. Snatch the Handkerchief
15. Silence
16. Smiles
17. Virginia Reel
18. Good Night Ladies

Directions for all these games may be found from the Index.

Plan to have about half of an evening's program rhythmical, for there is something invaluable in the combination of laughter and rhythm. The Grand March always starts the fun. No matter how uneven the number of men and girls, there is something so contagious about lines of young people—for they are all young in the Grand March—swinging up the room, that everyone from grandfather to wee Betsy wants to be part of it. The Grand March should not be merely a Grand March, it must be a *grand* march, and every figure should be a game. The popular and patriotic songs are the best, both for the rhythm and the spirit that is necessary in marching. Starting the Grand March with something they all love to sing will unconsciously swing the whole party into a spirit of pleasure. The very best music for this kind of party has proved to be piano and drum, rather than an orchestra or band.

Many of the games like Merry-Go-Round, Rig-a-Jig, Living Alphabet and Popularity may be used over again always with a new interest. Some new games are introduced at every party, however, and a stunt like "Wild Nell" is never repeated.

Almost every lively activity in which the whole group takes part is followed either by some event put on by two or more people, such as "This Is My Nose" or by a stunt, such as the "Suitcase Race."

The general singing takes up not more than fifteen minutes and includes patriotic songs, old favorites and funny songs such as "John Brown's Baby Has a Cold Upon Its Chest." This line is repeated twice and the last line is "And they rubbed it with camphorated oil." In the second verse, leave out the word "baby" and go through the motions of rocking a baby. In the third verse leave out the word "cold" and sneeze; in the fourth, leave out "chest," and each one slaps his chest; and in the last, leave out "rubbed," and each one rubs his chest.

Or sing "John Brown's Body," and each time leave out one more word; in the first verse, "grave;" the second verse, "the;" third verse, "in," etc., the leader going through strenuous "leading" motions during all the silences.

Another pantomime way of singing is to sing a song like "Smiles" leaving out the word "Smiles" in each case, smiling instead.

Singing contests between groups seated in different parts of the room are very successful.

The program is usually closed by the best game of the evening, when the fun is at the highest point. "Good Night, Ladies," sung with real feeling is most effective.

CHAPTER IV

Whistling Women

Four girls are asked to whistle one note. The one who holds her note the longest without taking breath gets a whistle for a prize.

Milk Bottle Race

Each contestant is given a baby's milk bottle. At a given signal they race to see which one can first drain his bottle of all the milk.

Darkness

Four or more players are given canes. Starting at one end of the room they walk to the other, tracing their paths with the canes. They are then blindfolded, turned around three times and told to retrace their steps with the aid of a cane.

Blind Chariot Race

Use three or four teams. Goal is pointed out before blindfolding. Each "team" is made up of two horses and a driver. All three are blindfolded and facing in the same direction; horses' inside arms are locked together. Driver takes hold of outside arms, each team is turned around three times, and at a signal, races to the goal.

Aviation Meet

Each team is made up of one aviator and two mechanics, and is given a string about fifty feet long and a cornucopia eight inches long, which is threaded lengthwise on the string. The two mechanicians hold the ends of each string, and the aviator blows the cornucopia from one end of the string to the other. The winner receives the blue ribbon.

Tug of War for Prunes

A prune is tied firmly in the middle of a long piece of twine, and each of the two contestants takes one end of the twine in his mouth and begins to chew his string for the prune. He is not allowed to use his hands.

Newspaper Race

Each contestant is given two newspapers, one for each foot. He places one newspaper in front of him and steps on it with the right foot. He then places the other for his left foot and so on, being allowed to step only on newspaper. The contestants race to a given mark and back.

Peanut Pass

Form in two facing lines. A pan of peanuts stands beside each leader, and an empty pan stands at the end of each line. Every one in each line clasps his neighbors' hands and must not once drop them. At a signal, the leader begins picking up the peanuts one at a time and passes them down the line as rapidly as possible. If a peanut is dropped, it must be picked up with the hands clasped. The side which first passes all its peanuts from one pan to the other gets all the peanuts.

Clothespins may be used instead of peanuts. They may be passed in the same way, or with the group standing in two columns, facing the front of the room, and passing the clothespins back over the heads.

Opera Glass Race

Contestants race along parallel chalk lines, looking through the large end of opera glasses.

Awkward Eating Race

1. Four or more apples are placed on the floor, on paper. The participants, who are on their knees, race in eating the apples without the aid of their hands.

2. Crackers are strung on strings suspended from a board. Contestants eat them, hands clasped behind.

3. Crackers are placed in mouths of contestants. They are to be eaten without using the hands.

Suitcase Race

Each contestant has a suitcase and an umbrella. In the suitcase are a hat, a coat, gloves, and any other clothing desired, so long as the contents are uniform. At a given signal, all contestants run to the goal, open suitcases, put on clothes, close suitcases, open umbrellas, and run to starting point. Use of the relay adds excitement.

Relay Races

In relay races there should be an equal number in the competing teams, and, unless otherwise stated, each team in a column, leaders facing the goal.

After the first one, or leader, of each line has started,

each one in his line is to wait until touched off, or until necessary implements are given to him. Touching off is done by the hands. A contestant when awaiting the touch off, shall toe the starting line with one foot and reach one hand directly forward as far as possible to meet that of the approaching toucher off. Each contestant, after having done his part and touched off the next one, shall go to the end of the line.

Indian Club

1. Have three Indian clubs on goal mark, for each line. First one runs up and knocks down clubs; second one puts them up; third knocks down, etc.

2. One circle at goal mark for each line, with three Indian clubs in each. First one puts clubs outside the circle; second one puts them inside; third outside, etc.

3. Have one club on goal mark for each line and give one club to each leader. First one exchanges her club with one at mark and brings it back to next girl who does the same.

In all these Indian Club Relays, if a club falls down, the runner must go back and pick it up.

The Lamplighter

Each contestant is given a lighted candle. The one who in the shortest time reaches a distant goal with his candle burning, wins. If the candle goes out, contestant must return to starting point to have it relighted. The relay plan may be used.

Hoops

Relay Formation, about six men in each team. The first man in each line is provided with a barrel hoop.

At a signal he raises it, pulls it down over his head, shoulders, and body, steps out of it and hands it to the one behind him, himself going to the end of the line at once. The object of each line is of course to draw itself through the hoops in the shortest time. It hardly detracts from the fun to have several stout people in the teams!

Bean Travel

Relay Formation. Each leader is provided with a bean and a spoon. The object is to push the bean, by means of the spoon, to the goal and back. As soon as he has finished, he hands the bean and spoon to the one behind him and goes immediately to the end of the line.

Cracker Relay Race

Relay Formation. Each one supplied with a cracker. At the signal, the first one in each row begins to eat his cracker. As soon as he can whistle, after eating his cracker, the next one begins. The row which finishes first must give one long whistle in unison.

The same idea may be used with apples. Each leader is given an apple. First one pares an apple; the second one cuts it in halves; the third one quarters it and cuts out the core; the fourth one eats it.

Water Drinking Relay

Sixteen is a good number for this game, eight men and eight girls. Each man has a partner, and they stand in two double lines. Each girl is provided with a tumbler half full of water, and a teaspoon. At a given signal, the two girls who head the two respective lines begin to feed their partners the water, using the teaspoon. As soon as either couple finishes, they must sing together the first verse and chorus of Yankee Doodle, at the end of which the next couple begins to do away with the water. The side which finishes first marches around the other side singing Yankee Doodle.

Wind

Place lighted candles on a table at the end of a room. First one in each line stands in front of one candle, is then blindfolded, takes three steps backwards, is turned around three times and then advances three steps and tries to blow out the candle. As soon as he succeeds, the bandage is taken from his eyes, and he touches off the next blower.

Potato Race

About six potatoes are laid in four or more rows a yard apart. Contestants run to first potato, pick it up with a spoon, place it in a basket at the starting point, pick up the second, then the third, until all have been picked up. They are quickly placed again in the same position by contestants, and the next runner does the same thing. Usually there are three in a team. A knife may be used instead of a spoon. Peanuts may be used instead of potatoes, and they may be carried either on knives or on the back of the left hand.

The Draft

A fan and a piece of tissue paper are given each person. The object of the race is by means of the fan to blow the tissue paper to the goal and back.

Folding Chair Relay

Eight couples of a large group are placed in groups of two couples each, one couple standing behind the other, the entire group about twenty feet from a goal line. The first man of each group carries a folding chair unopened. His partner takes his arm and must keep it throughout the race. At a signal, each first couple runs to the goal line, where the man opens the chair, places it, seats his partner in it, helps her up, folds the chair, and together they run back to touch off the next couple. There may be several variations to this; for example, walk instead of run; walk backwards; man stands on chair and together they count twenty; girl must sing chorus of some popular song to partner.

Couple Relays

The formation for the next seven relays is like that for the Folding Chair Race, except, of course, that the man does not carry a chair. Partners go through each event together, arms locked. Goals may be about thirty feet away.

1. Walk.
2. Two step.
3. Hippity-hop.
4. Hop on one foot.
5. Walk backward.
6. With beanbag on head (if one beanbag falls off, both must stoop to pick it up).
7. Skipping.

NOTE: To choose winner.—Sometimes there are four or five people who come out first in a contest. To decide which one gets the prize, have each one open a book in turn. Note the first letter on the page. The one whose first letter is nearest the beginning of the alphabet wins.

Blindfolding.—Whenever blindfolding is necessary, use strip of gauze with pieces of absorbent cotton as blinders. These pieces are fastened to the gauze with adhesive plaster.

CHAPTER V

TRICKS

The following activities are particularly useful for filling in between activities in which the entire group has taken part—rest periods, so to speak. These may be used for either large or small groups.

The Battle

Two men are seated on the floor, facing each other. They are told that they are to be blindfolded and that each one will be given a "swatter" made of newspaper—with which to take turns at hitting each other. Only one of them is blindfolded!

Cahoots

Two people who have a secret understanding engineer this game. One who is blindfolded kneels, facing the group. The other stands behind him, and the following conversation takes place: "Are you in Cahoots with me?" "Yes." "Do you point as I point?" (pointing at some one). "Yes." "Do you point as I point?" "Yes." "At whom am I pointing?" and the kneeling one answers, always correctly. The one pointed at is the last one who spoke before the question, "Are you in Cahoots with me?"

The Vicious Ring

Five or six people are asked to leave the room and come in one at a time. A ring is hung on a nail in the wall. The victim is asked to fix his sense of direction before being blindfolded, when he is to try to put his forefinger through the ring. He advances towards the wall blindfolded, and just before he reaches it the jaws of a toy alligator snap on his finger. The blindfolding bandage usually comes off in a hurry.

Mental Telepathy

The group is told that if a group of people think hard enough about an object they have chosen, they can communicate the thought to a person who knows nothing about it. One or two "unwise" persons are asked to leave the room. Nothing is decided upon, but the group is told that when each "unwise" person comes in in turn, they must appear to be concentrating. No matter what he guesses to be the object, great disappointment is shown, and he is urged to guess again. Whatever he chooses the second time is conceded to be the right thing, and he is heartily congratulated on his success. This continues until he realizes he is being duped. It is wise to vary the plan, having the second object the right one for a time, then perhaps the first, then the fourth, etc.

Concentration

Claim that you can go out of a room, while the group decides upon four words which are to be written on a slip of paper. If they will concentrate on those four words, you, on coming into the room, can easily write the same thing. You proceed to do so, handing your paper to some reliable person, asking him quietly to read them and then inform the group as to whether or not you have written the same thing. In each case you have. What you wrote of course was "The same thing."

Black Magic

Announce that this is an initiation. Several people are sent out of the room and brought in blindfolded one at a time, facing the rest of the group. Three plates are put before the victim. One contains water, one is empty, and the other has smut on the bottom of it. He is told to put his finger in the first plate and perform mystic signs on his face. Then he is told to rub his finger on the bottom of the second, doing the same, and last on the bottom of the one containing the smut. He is then given a seat in the audience before the bandage is taken from his eyes, so that his first intimation of his own decorative appearance comes when he sees the other fellow, receiving the initiation.

I See a Ghost

Five or six courageous spirits who are professedly not afraid of ghosts form a single line facing the audience, shoulder to shoulder. The first one says in sepulchral tones, "I see a ghost." The next one asks "Where?" and the first one answers, "Over there," pointing with her right hand. The second one tells the third one, and so on down the line, the last one telling the first all about it. This continues, pointing next with the left hand, then kneeling on the right knee, and then the left knee until all in the line are pointing outward with both hands and are on their knees. The final move is for the first one to push the entire line over.

Reading Temples

Two people with a previous understanding work together in this. The group is told by one of them that thoughts can be transmitted through the temples. He then leaves the room while the others decide on a number not greater than ten. The temple-reader is called in and feels several temples, remarking "No transmission there," etc., and at last triumphantly exclaims, "There! You gave it to me!" and putting the blame on some entirely innocent person. He is told the number by the grinding of his co-worker's teeth.

You without Me

The director stands before the group and invites them all to become members of the Altruistic Society. To do so, however, they must say the pass word "You without me" exactly as the leader says it. He points to one individual after another, asking them to try it, but in each case he says "You without me" in a different tone, sometimes singing it, or saying it in a high squeaky voice, often accompanying it with movements of the arms, facial contortions, etc. The one to whom he points must try to do it exactly as he did it. Finally some bright mind discovers that the thing to say is just "You," without "me," and without any of the elaborations.

The Telltale Glass

Invert a tumbler and place it on a table; then ask some one to lend you a coin. Place the coin on top of the glass. You leave the room, telling the company at the same time that if a person will take the penny and conceal it, you will tell them when you return which person has it. Someone having concealed the coin, you make your appearance and request each one around the table to place his first finger on the glass, one after another. This done, you take up the glass and place it to your ear, remarking at the same time that by the aid of the sound that you hear you will be able to tell which person has the coin. Then you listen for a second or two, put down the glass and turning to the person who has the coin, make some remark such as "Mr. Blank, please give me the penny," whereupon the person addressed produces the coin and hands it to you. Of course you have learned who he is through your confederate, who placed his finger on the glass after the person who had the coin.

The Elusive Dime

Take one of the old coinage of dimes with a good clear milling around the edge. Press it on some one's forehead. Remove your hand and allow him to shake his head and see if he can shake the dime off. If pressed firmly, it will stick and will be hard to shake off. The individual of course must not wrinkle his forehead. After several have been given a trial, carefully remove the dime from the next man's head after pressing it firmly on his forehead. He immediately starts to shake his head, thinking the dime is still there.

The Hungry Blind

Two men sit on the floor, blindfolded, their clothing protected by many newspapers. They feed each other ice-cream, usually making vain and disastrous attempts to reach each other's mouths.

Cock-a-doodle-doo

The leader whispers to each one, supposedly giving to each the name of the animal he is to imitate. Instead, he tells all to keep silent except one, who is to crow lustily. He then counts *one, two, three,* and the rooster crows while all the dumb animals laugh at him.

Aeroplane Ride

Those who are to take the trip are blindfolded before they enter the room in turn. A strong board is held, an inch or so from the floor, by two or more persons. A blindfolded girl is asked to step on the board, and told to put her hands on the shoulders of a girl who steers. The board is raised a little and then, instead of raising it higher the one in front stoops down by degrees, and the girl taking the trip, feeling the shoulders going down, imagines that the board is being raised higher and higher until she finally feels that she must be perilously near the ceiling. Finally the steerer tells her to let go her shoulders. Then the ''conductors'' tell her to jump when they count three, but not to be afraid, as she will land on a mattress. It is great sport to see her prepare for an attempt to execute an enormous jump and land in a heap, after falling two inches. An egg beater, worked vigorously to imitate the sound of the machinery and fanning the rider, adds to the effect.

Quartet

Four people are taken out of the room. One is ''unwise'' and does not know the trick. They are told that they are to sing a song of four words, the sentence to contain the word ''sold.'' The ''unwise'' one is as-

signed that word. The tune is practiced with all singing. When they come out to sing, the victim alone sings
"sold."

The Mystic Book

A blindfolded victim is told that he is privileged to
kiss the Mystic Book three times, through which privilege he will gain the gift of beauty. He does this twice,
but the third time a saucer of flour has been placed inside the cover.

The Paper Artist

One of two confederates leaves the room. The other,
with plenty of tablet paper at hand, pretends to make
an impression of some subject's face on a piece of paper,
by pressing it gently around the nose, eyes and mouth.
He calls in his confederate who tells him at once, on
looking at the paper, whose picture the artist took. He
does this by noticing his confederate's hands, which are
held exactly like those of the subject. This continues,
using fresh paper each time until someone catches on.

The Mysterious Bags

Five or more paper bags are tied to a pole which may
be held by two tall men. Peanuts are in one of the bags,
candy in another, sawdust in another, water in a water-
proof sack, and a little pepper in another. Five men
are blindfolded. Each one in turn is given a short stick
and is led up to the pole, told to turn around, and then
given three tries at hitting the bags. If he breaks the
candy bag, he gets the candy, if the water bag, the
water! If all the bags are not broken when the five

men have had their turns, call out as many more as are necessary, until all the bags are broken. Of course no one knows anything about the contents of the bags.

The One-Eyed Dressmaker

If in a large group, from five to ten men are sent to a dark room; if the group is small, all the men are sent. They are brought out one at a time and each one is asked if he can thread a needle with one eye closed. They are always sure they can! The victim is seated, given a piece of fine thread and a needle with a large eye, one that would not be the least bit difficult to thread. His right eye is closed for him by someone who stands behind him, covering the eye with a hand, which incidentally has lamp black on it. When he has successfully threaded the needle he is duly praised and then sent back to the darkened room, until all the other men have gone through the same performance. They are brought into the lighted room together. Each one enjoys immensely the somewhat sooty eye of the other fellow!

Powerful Vision

A confederate is necessary, one who has been told to write a certain word, "Kitchener" perhaps. The leader tells the group that if each guest will write the name of something on a slip of paper and fold it, and then let him rub it across his forehead, he can tell what each one wrote. The slips are collected and given to the leader who takes them one by one, folded as they are, rubs them across the forehead, tells what is written on each one, opens it to confirm it, and as he does so asks the one who wrote it to raise his hand. In each case he is correct of course! His method is simple. After rub-

bing the first slip across his forehead he says "Kitchener," and his confederate raises his hand. In the meanwhile the leader has read what was written on the first
slip, and he calls that out, for the second slip. Then,
of course what was written on the second slip he gives
for the third, etc., etc. After all the slips have been read,
they may be passed around for the group to read, that
each one might have proof of the vision of the leader!

Copy Cat

There are a great many of these copy cat tricks, in
which the group is asked to repeat what the leader says,
and say it in the same way. Her statement may be
"American girls are very fine girls," and she may change
the inflection of her voice each time, whereas in reality
the trick is that she cleared her throat before each statement. The group usually sits in a circle and in turn
each one mimics the leader, who tells them when they
are "initiated." This continues until each one has it.

Magic

There are in addition a great many means by which a
leader who has a confederate may know what object has
been decided upon during his absence. When the leader
comes in, his confederate may name several objects, each
time receiving "No" as an answer until he mentions a
four-legged object which they had previously decided
should always precede the object chosen; they might use
the name of something black; something which flies;
something which cuts. Any of these may precede the
chosen object, so long as there is an understanding between the confederates.

Hawaiian Puzzle

Three rows of books are placed on the floor. There may be any number greater than three in each row. The leader sends her confederate out of the room while some one in the group points to any book. The leader calls in her confederate, points to various books asking "Is it this?" "Is it that?" coughing, changing her position, and the inflection of her voice, and in every way leading the group to believe that it is something she does which tells the confederate which book it is each time. The leader allows them to try out all their theories as to the solution, but finally it boils down to the fact that the trick lies in the use of "this" or "that." After that it seems simple. They invariably think it has to do with numbers—the third "that" after two "this-es!" etc. The leader can easily explode every theory! for example, someone might say "It is the first 'that,' after two 'this-es,' " so the next time the leader says, "Is it this?" pointing to the right book the very first time, her confederate, of course, saying "Yes."

This is the understanding between the leader and her confederate. The rows of books are called, "This," "That" and "This," the middle row "That" and the two outside rows "This." Suppose a book in the middle row is the one chosen. It is of course in the "That" row. The leader might point to two or three in a "This" row, saying in each case, "Is it this?" her confederate answering in the negative. The leader might then point to one or two books in the "That" row asking, "Is it that?" again getting a negative answer. But let her point to a book in the *"That"* row and ask, "Is it *this?*" her confederate will know at once it is the chosen book. Or if she points to a book in a *"This"* row and asks, "Is it *that?"* it will be the right book.

One group of college men and women worked on this puzzle for almost two years before they solved it. It seems simple!

Brother, I'm Bobbed

Two men sit side by side. Their laps are covered with some sort of robe, which is large enough to be pulled over the head. One of them knows the trick, and he has a "swatter" made of folded newspaper concealed at his side. The leader tells them that some one of the guests standing very close to them, will strike them, one at a time. The one hit must throw off the covering immediately and guess who hit him. Of course, it is the "wise one" who does the hitting, immediately concealing the stick, sometimes giving himself a sounding whack to dupe his companion further.

Gentlemen Nursemaids

Several girls who know the trick act as "artists." Four or more men are seated facing the audience. Each one is blindfolded and is asked to double up his right fist. Upon the back of the fist each artist makes the mouth, nose and eyes of a face with burnt cork or a little water color. A doll's cap, a lace frill, or a muslin ruffle is tied around this and a full white apron or skirt is fastened around the wrist. The left arm is bent to lie across the chest and the right wrist put into the inner bend of the elbow, drawing the apron down over the right arm. Each of the blindfolded men will appear to be tenderly holding a baby. Have the blindfolds removed.

Faith, Hope, and Charity

Some of the men are sent from the room. Three girls named Faith, Hope, Charity stand behind chairs which conceal a man, preferably one with a beard. The men are brought in one by one and told that if they will choose one of the girls they will get a kiss. No matter which one they choose, they are seated in the middle chair, are blindfolded, and the man in the rear kisses them.

Blind Obstacle Race

Obstacles such as vases of flowers, china-ware, footstools, cushions, etc., are placed in four or more long rows. Each contestant is given a row and is requested to try distances before being blindfolded. They are all then blindfolded, are placed at the starting point and told to race, each one through his line of obstacles without touching anything. Meanwhile, the objects have been removed.

CHAPTER VI

GAMES

Formations for Games

Where the formation calls for two lines facing, partners side by side, as in Living Alphabet and Animated Adjectives, if a large group, use the Grand March to get the guests into lines four abreast, a man, a girl, a man and a girl, etc., facing the director. Divide the group down the middle, asking each division to form a single line facing the center, man standing to the right (or left) of partner. If sets are required, have the lines count off by sixes or eights or tens, each group forming a set.

For dividing a large group into single circles in which partners stand side by side, come up in eights. The one on the right end of each line counts for his line. Lines count off by twos. Lines number one face lines number two and spread out, taking hold of hands and forming circles of sixteen each. To make several double circles, ask the girls to step inside the circles in front of their partners.

For getting a large group into one big double circle, use the Grand March and come up in twos. Leading couple marches to right, all other couples following and forming a large double circle. To make one large single circle, have men step to the right of their partners.

71

Musical Games

The group activities which may be done to the accompaniment of music include folk-dances, musical games, square dances and figure marching, which have been so adapted that they are easy to use with a large group of men and girls, and are enjoyed by large groups. They can be used equally well for groups of twenty or thirty or for groups of two or three hundred. Whenever possible, it makes the work of the director, when working with a large group, much lighter, if ten or twelve sub-directors who know each game thoroughly can be scattered about through the group. Unless the girls know the words to the singing games, it is never advisable to try to teach them to a large group. A whistle for each change of step is more effective. A quick and easy way to get members of a large group into position for folk-dances, etc., is to use the Grand March, and divide and place the different groups as desired.

Grand March Figures

Fall in, in two separate columns, men in one and the girls in the other. The following directions are based on the assumption that two columns, one of men and one of girls, face the director.

Figure I.   The Bridge

1. Lines separate, leaders taking them to the other end of the room where the two lines meet and come up double (with partners). 2. Stay with partners, first couple going to right, second to left, third to right. 3. Come up in fours. 4. Divide in twos again. 5. When these two lines of twos meet at the far end of the room, the line at the director's right forms a bridge by

holding inside hands high, while the other line passes
under it, both lines marching all the while. When they
again meet at director's end of the room, the other side
forms bridges, and the former bridges pass under. This
is done twice, both sides forming bridges two times.
Either fast-time or skipping-step music adds a great deal
to the fun.

Figure II. The Pivot

Come up in fours. The three to the right of each line
of four pivot right, leaving one on left to march alone to
the left. Come up in fours. Three to left of each line
pivot left, leaving one at right to march alone to right.
Come up in fours.

Figure III. The Merry-Go-Round

Fours divide into twos, going to right and left. When
the two lines approach each other at far end of room,
the leading couple of each line takes eight counts, counting aloud, to meet leading couple of other line, while
rest of group stands still. On eight these four join hands
in a circle and skip seven counts to left. On the eighth
count the two from the left line pop under a bridge
formed by the right line couple, each couple going forward in eight counts to meet the next couple of the opposite line. Repeat until leading couples again meet. Break
ranks.

Figure IV. Countermarch

Each leader turns back close upon his own line, turning always away from center at each end of the room.
When lines are widely separated, leaders at far end of
the room, bring lines to center and come up in twos.

Figure V. Interlacing

First couple to right, second to left, etc. When the two lines meet at far end of room, men of left column step inside, men of right column step outside and march on. Girls of left column march next to men of right column, while girls of right column march next to men of left column. Make complete circle of room twice. Come up in fours.

Figure VI. Snake Dance

Fours right and left. Come up in eights and halt with plenty of space between lines. The leader is the one at the right end of the front line. Hands held across each line. Leader with first line skips into winding formation, leading her line so that attachment can be made with line that is waiting. Attachment can be made only between last one of skipping line and one to extreme right of waiting line. When entire group is in line, after skipping along a twisted path, break ranks.

Figure VII. London Bridge

Come up in fours; inside two join hands, outside two march forward, meet, and go under bridge. When they come to other end separate and come up in former places. Each bridge in turn follows the last couple through, turns away from center and comes up on far side of partner.

These figures may be used separately or in a group of two or three figures at a time, or sometimes even as one entire group, but that is hardly advisable because smaller groups of figures serve splendidly at intervals during an evening's recreation. It is always effective to begin and close an evening with a Grand March.

"We Won't Go Home until Morning"

Music, "We Won't Go Home until Morning." The verse is played twice, then the chorus.

Use the Grand March to form two parallel lines which face each other, partners opposite. Each group may contain as many as twenty couples.

Hands are clasped along the lines. Lines are called left or right, being determined left or right by director's position.

1. Three walking steps forward and bob to partner. (1-2-3-bob).

2. Three steps backward and bob (1-2-3-bob).

3. Lines marching, cross over, exchanging places in following manner: Those of right line hold hands high, while those of left line drop hands and pass under these hands held high, passing to partner's *right*. This may be done in seven short steps, on count eight facing about and bowing, standing in partner's place.

4. Repeat 1, all holding hands along lines.

5. Repeat 2.

6. Repeat 3.

Chorus

1. Clap hands (1-2-3-pause).

2. Repeat.

3. Partners hook right elbows and skip in circle 8 counts.

4. Partners hook left elbows and skip in circle 8 counts, each one running back to his partner's place on the 8th count. Repeat from beginning, each one going to his own place on the last count.

Popularity

Music, "Turkey in the Straw." Verse only, repeated over and over. Whistle is blown at end of verse, or at unexpected intervals.

This game is invaluable where there are more men than girls or *vice versa*. Assuming that there are more men, all the men bunch in the middle of the room, the girls circle around them in as large a circle as possible, faced for marching, which means always with left hand on inside of circle. At a command, every man who can, takes a girl for his partner. The rest stay in the center. The men and girls forming the double circle march around until a whistle blows. Men then about-face and march in the opposite direction, while the girls continue marching forward. At a second whistle, all the men including those from the center jump to get a partner. The left-overs are not allowed to leave the circle but must go to the center and wait for the next chance. The marching continues as before. This is one of the most popular games for large groups.

Merry-Go-Round

Music, "Merry-Go-Round."

Formation—double circle, partners facing. Hands on hips.

1. Hop on left foot pointing right toe directly to side, change quickly to right foot, pointing left toe to side alternating rapidly. This continues through measure 4. A whistle at that point may be the signal for change in step.

2. Hop on left foot, pointing right toe forward,

changing quickly to right foot and alternating all through measure 6.

3. Stamp 1-2-3, 1-2-3, 1-2-3-4-5. Measures 7 and 8. Measures 9 to 16: All face center, inner circle joining hands, those outside putting hands on partner's shoulders. They imitate a merry-go-round, which goes very slowly at first, then faster and faster until it spins. The inside circle must be kept small, or disaster is inevitable! The step is a slide (to the right always) long and slow, at first, then rapidly becoming faster. At the end, partners change places, repeating from beginning.

Nigarepolska

Count number of players in circle. Take out a number of players, which number goes evenly into the whole number. For instance, if there are twenty-four in the circle, take out either two, four, or six players. They face any one they choose, a man facing a girl, etc. Every one has hands on hips and hops four times to music, hopping first on the left foot and touching the right heel to the floor, change, etc. At chorus those on the inside of the circle jump about, facing center, clapping hands once, then folding arms. Those whom they faced place hands on their shoulders. They run around the circle, counter clock-wise keeping close to the outer ring, in short running steps. At end of chorus they stop in front of the one closest at hand, and still in that same position all do the hop step. At chorus, hands are dropped from shoulders and those inside the circle jump around facing center, *each in his own place,* and the one whom they faced joins their line by placing his hands on the shoulders of the back one. This makes three in every line. This is repeated, and the train has four units, then five and so on, until every one has been chosen for some line, each line adding to itself only one person at a time. When the last ones have been chosen, the lines are all united by all leaders putting hands on the shoulders of the last one of the line ahead. The music is played faster and faster until the circle breaks.

Circus Horse

The formation is just as in "Popularity," except that all face the center, with the girls seated as far apart as possible and their men partners standing behind them. The surplus men or girls are in the center. The pianist plays different kinds of music which indicate the step to be used. If she plays a march, all the men who are standing behind chairs must face for marching and march around until, when the music stops suddenly, all the men rush for partners. Those who get left go to the center. The excitement comes in the suddenness with which the music stops. It may be necessary to have a girl leader to call out and perhaps demonstrate the various steps called for by the music. These steps may include a Run, March, Tip-toe, High step, Gallop, Fly, and Hippity-hop.

Rig a Jig Jig

Music, "Rig a Jig Jig," in "The Most Popular College Songs." Verse only, repeated over and over. Whistle is blown at end of each verse.

Form a large single circle, drop hands and step back. Any number, varying according to the size of the circle but usually from two for a small circle to ten for a large one, are chosen to step inside the ring and march around counter clockwise, close to the outer ring till first whistle blows. They then take the girl or man, nearest them as partner, cross hands as in skating, and go skipping around the circle close to the outside ring till the next whistle. All those who have been skipping drop hands and march around in single file. At whistle, they take partners from outside circle. When all have been chosen and have partners, the director calls out "Change partners," or whistles frequently, the players all the while skipping in a circle, catching new partners at every signal.

Jerusalem

The music should be lively march music and full of surprises. The principle of the 1919 model is exactly the same as that of the 1862 model with this exception, that girls or men may be substituted for chairs. About ten girls may substitute for chairs, standing in a column. Count off in twos down the line; No. 1's about-face so that along the entire column No. 1's face No. 2's, and each one stands with right hand on hip. Eleven or more men line up around them, march when the music starts, and when it stops most unexpectedly they scramble for an outstretched elbow. The left-over man and one girl are removed from the line of players each time.

Noriu Miego

Music, Noriu Miego, played more quickly each time the dance is repeated.

Used by permission of Clayton F. Summy Company, owners of copyright.

Form in sets of fours, all facing center of square Ladies opposite, gentlemen opposite.

1. Ladies, hands on hips; gentlemen, arms folded on chest. Hop on left foot and place right foot forward. Hop on right foot and place left foot forward. (2 counts for each change.) Measures 1 and 2. Hop on left foot and place right foot forward. Hop on right foot and place left foot forward. Hop on left foot and place right foot forward. (1 count for each change.) Measures 3 and half of measure 4. Rest remainder of measure 4.

2. All clap hands once. Ladies join right hands, gentlemen join right hands. All circle with seven walking steps. Turn about on seventh step. Measures 1 to 4 inclusive. All clap hands once. Circle in opposite direction with left hands joined. Measures 5 to 8 inclusive.

Forced Generosity

Formation, double circle, men outside. Assuming that there are more girls than men, extra girls in center. When music starts, all couples march around in circle, and the extra girls count the couples marching starting the count anywhere. Each one counts to five, and the girl of the fifth couple gives up her partner, going into the center. Music is continuous, but it is a good plan to call often for a reverse in the march.

Virginia Reels

The most suitable music is "Turkey in the Straw," "Whistling Rufus," "Morning Si" and "Pop Goes the Weasel."

For a very large new group, it is advisable to have either a sub-director or two leaders who know the figures thoroughly, for each group. To get them into position have all the men and girls get into two separate lines behind their respective leaders. The leaders separate, leading their lines down the opposite sides of the room, meet in center of the far end and come up with partners. Directors go rapidly down line counting couples off by six, sending the groups of twelve to various parts of the room. The two lines of six separate and face each other in parallel lines. The players clap hands in time with the music.

The people at the right ends of each line are called diagonal right leaders; left ends, diagonal left leaders. Each movement of diagonal right leaders is repeated by diagonal left leaders. Right leaders begin.

1. Come to center and bow.
2. Swing round right hands.
3. Swing round left hands.
4. Swing round both hands.
5. Do-Si-Do.— Arms folded high. Go round each other at center, back to back.
6. All four leaders come to center, clasp right hands across and swing round once.

The partners opposite each other at the heads of the lines now lead the figures.

7. Hands on partner'~ shoulders, dance down center and back.
8. Swing partner with right elbows locked.
9. Swing first one of partner's line, left elbows locked.
10. Swing partner—right elbows.
11. Swing second one of partner's line, left elbows locked.
12. Swing partner.

This continues until leaders have swung each one of partner's line. Leaders then dance down center, hands on each other's shoulders, to their places at the heads of their own lines. Each one leads his own line, turning away from center, to where last couple of group had stood. There leaders join hands forming a bridge, under which all pass with partners, first pair through taking position of head couple, and the original first couple remain where they formed bridge, taking position of last couple. This continues until original first couple gets back to place.

Barn-Dance

Music, "Morning Si."

In the barn-dance there are two steps which are used throughout.

Step No. 1. Three short running steps and hop (step—step—step—hop). This step is always done twice.

Step No. 2. Step—hop, step—hop, step—hop, step—hop.

New barn-dance figures are very easily formed, using the two different steps as a foundation. The following are some suggestions for figures. The lady is always at the gentleman's right. In using any of these figures, they are repeated over and over until the music stops.

Figure I. Position, facing forward, inside hands joined.

Step No. 1. Partners go forward.

Step No. 2. Lady crosses diagonally in front of man and back to place, man doing step hop in place.

Repeat Step No. 1.

Step No. 2. Gentleman crosses diagonally and back.

Figure II. Position, partners face, gentleman going backwards, hands on shoulders.

Step No. 1. Go in direction lady is facing.

Step No. 2. Slowly reverse positions.

Step No. 1. Go in direction gentleman is facing.

Step No. 2. Reverse.

Figure III Position, both facing forward holding hands crossed as in skating, right hands on top.

Step No. 1. Forward.

Step No. 2. Raise arms, not dropping hands, lady turning away from partner toward her right, makes a complete circle, man doing step-hop in place.

Step No. 1. Forward.

Step No. 2. Man makes circle, turning away from partner to his left.

Figure IV. Position, in fours. Partners face forward, the two front ones joining inside hands only, giving outside hands to the other two in same position back of them.

Step No. 1. Forward.

Step No. 2. Back two step-hop in place keeping hold of hands. First two drop inside front hands only and turning away from each other step-hop around the other two, until they meet behind them. They join hands, and the formation is now with the original front couple in the rear and the original back couple in the front.

Step No. 1. Forward.

Step No. 2. Exactly like Step No. 2 above, the front couple separating and going to rear.

Family Virginia Reel

The unique feature of this Virginia Reel is that the entire group, by couples, performs figures at the same time. Formation—two parallel lines facing each other; partners opposite.

1. Each side joins hands along line. Lines come to center, bow and back. Repeat.

2. Lines drop hands; each couple performs first five figures given above, all couples going through the figures at same time.

3. All follow leaders who march, each line turning away from center, to the place where the last couple had stood. There leaders join hands, forming a bridge. As each couple passes under it, they too join hands forming a bridge, until the last couple has passed under. Repeat from the beginning.

Couple Virginia Reel

Group comes up in fours. Divide in middle, each side forming single line facing center, standing man, girl, man, girl, etc. Count off by fours making eight in each set.

1. Each set holds hands along lines—advance and bow—repeat. Drop hands. Partners do succeeding steps together, diagonal right couples leading and diagonal left couples following.

2. First five steps of Virginia Reel given above.

(Note:—Man of one couple swings girl of opposite couple.)

3. Join right hands in center—swing 8 steps around.

4. Repeat left hands.

Follow leaders, who march away from center to where last couple of set stood, where they meet, forming a bridge under which other couples pass, first pair through taking position of head couple, original leaders remaining where they formed bridge. Repeat with new partners.

NOTE:—There is almost no limit to one's resources for finding and adapting material of the kind suggested in this chapter. The above are merely examples of the type of activity most effective, and the adaptations necessary. In choosing material of this kind it is essential that all of it be simple enough to give the maximum amount of pleasure to a group.

Bibliography for Musical Games

For Folk Dances:

"Folk Dances and Singing Games," by Elizabeth Burchenal. Schirmer, New York, $1.50.

"Hinman Gymnastic Dancing," Volume III, by Mary Wood Hinman.

"Lithuanian Folk Dances," by Helen Rich Shipps. Clayton Summy Company, Chicago, 40 cents.

For Figure Marching:

"Cotillion Figures," by Watkins. Neal Publishing Company, New York. $1.00.

For Square Dances, such as "Old Dan Tucker," "Money Musk," etc.:

"Polite and Social Dances," by Mari Ruef Hofer, Clayton Summy Company, Chicago. $1.00.

Songs:

"The Most Popular College Songs," Hinds, Hayden and Eldridge, New York. 50 cents.

Games for Large Groups

The following games are particularly good for large groups, but any one of them can be used for smaller groups.

Puzzle Words

Write out words and then cut them up into single letters, giving the same number to each letter of a given word. For example, in the word "battle," number each letter of "battle" 1. All the Number Ones are told to get together, discover what their word is and when their number is called, act it out for the group to guess. As many as fifty words may be given out.

In a similar manner, proverbs can be cut up, put together and then acted out.

Living Alphabet

Formation—two lines facing, partners side by side. Two differently colored sets of the alphabet are given out, one to each line. In playing this with a small group, if there are not enough guests to have twenty-six in each line, two, three, or even four letters may be given to one person. The leader calls out words, easy at first, and those from each group holding the letters making up that word must run out and form the word, each one holding his letter high, and facing the judges. If a letter is used twice in a word the holder must go first to one place and then to the other. In case of a double letter holder needs only to jiggle his letter back and forth. The judges decide which side forms the word first, and a score is kept. Eleven is usually the score limit. Judges should be so placed that the audience can easily see the formations of the words.

White Elephant

Guests have been asked to bring some article for which they have no further use, wrapped in white tissue paper. (At one White Elephant Party, a bachelor brought five crocheted neckties and two pairs of fancy bedroom slippers.) These undesirables are exchanged unopened. The recipients open the packages and if they are not satisfied, they re-wrap the articles and continue exchanging until satisfied.

Animated Adjectives

Formation—Two lines, A and B facing, partners side by side. No definite number is necessary, and this game may be played with as few as five to ten on each side. The two lines are the width of the room apart. The leader of each line assigns a letter to the people in her line. Each side then mixes up its letters so that "a" may stand next to "t," "b" next to "q," or "m" next to "x." The first person on A's side may be *f*. F walks over to the other line and back, acting out an adjective beginning with *f;* and if B's side does not guess that he is acting out "Foolish," for instance, thereby guessing his adjective and letter before he gets back, he is safe. If they do guess, he belongs to B. Then the first one on B's side acts his adjective, the next one on A's side, and so forth. A count is taken at the end, and the side having won the most enemies may demand forfeits of the other side.

Games for Either Large or Small Groups

In using the following games for large groups, it is always advisable to divide them into smaller groups; if for circle formation, then several small circles, and if for two lines facing, divide them into sets.

Bobby-de-Bob

Formation—Circles made up of not more than fifteen people with one person in the center. Each one is given a number larger than ten. The one in the center points to some one very unexpectedly; and if she says "Bobby-de-bob," the one pointed at must say his number immediately, but if she says nothing, silence should be forthcoming. The penalty for a mistake is to exchange places with the one in the center. The joy of this game is the bewilderment of the one pointed at, especially if the pointer is quick and unexpected in her movements.

Silence

The funniest imaginable story is told and a forfeit demanded on the least suggestion of a laugh or a smile.

Lightning

The company is divided into two groups. One person is chosen from each side to leave the room while both sides decide on a common letter. The two are then called in, at a signal they are told the letter, and immediately they must call out every word they know which begins with that letter, score keepers keeping score of the number of words. They are allowed two minutes. Usually they are so confused that stuttering takes up the first minute and a half.

Grand Opera

Formation—Circles, with one person in the center. If a large group is being entertained divide it into several circles, with ten to fifteen in each circle. One in center is blindfolded and carries a cane. Those forming the circle march around singing a popular song until the blindfolded person calls "Halt." He then, with his cane, points to someone in the circle who must grasp the end of the cane and sing the chorus of any song the blindfolded person names. If his voice is recognized he must go in the center. Names are not necessary in guessing identities, especially in a large group. "The man with the bright red hair," or "The girl who led the Grand March," will suffice.

Unknown Stunt

Like "Magic Music," except that the victim must perform some stunt decided by the group, such as climbing over a chair. He must keep on doing stunts until the music shows he has done the right one.

Smiles

Formation—Two lines facing, partners opposite. If a large group, have them grand march and come up in twos. Director counts off by sixes, placing sets of six couples in various parts of room, lines facing. The girls try every conceivable way of making the men smile or laugh. Any man who does must come to the girls' line. After about five minutes of this every man in a girl's line must pay a forfeit.

Betsy

Formation—Circle, with one in center, "Betsy," whose eyes are blindfolded. This being done, the other players hastily change places so as to put her memory of their arrangement at fault. Then she walks around the circle and points to someone. The person to whom she is pointing must give Betsy both hands and then sing up and down the scale once. If Betsy guesses who it is the warbler changes places with her, but if, on the contrary, she makes a wrong guess, the company warns her of it by clapping their hands and she passes on to someone else. The leader may give hints as to the identity of the person whose name is to be guessed.

Peanut Hunt

Peanuts are hidden in every conceivable place. At a signal, the group is told to search for them and keep them for the count. The player who has the most is given a toy pig.

Spontaneous Dramatics

Out of a large group are taken two or three small groups. While some other activity is going on they are given five minutes in which to prepare to stage some nursery story. For instance, the first group might be assigned "Red Riding Hood." The parts are given out, impromptu costumes are gathered, and the play goes on. The action is all in pantomime and the name of the play is not announced, the audience guessing it from the acting.

Mother Goose rhymes may be used the same way.

Hiram and Mirandy

A man is chosen for Hiram, and a girl for Mirandy. They go inside the circle, where Hiram is blindfolded. He calls sharply, "Mirandy." She answers sweetly, "Yes, Hiram," whereupon he dashes in the direction the voice came from, trying to catch her, she, of course, eluding him. He calls constantly and she must answer at once, never leaving the circle. When he catches her she chooses a Hiram and he chooses a Mirandy.

Animal Alphabet

The group is divided into two lines which face. The first person on one side names an animal the name of which begins with "a." The first one on the second side names another, and so on until one side is at the end of its resources and can't name any more. That side gives up one of its players to the opposite side. The losing side begins with "b," and then "c," and so on, having a time limit. The side with the greatest number of players wins.

New York and Boston

Two captains choose alternately till all have been chosen. The sides line up facing each other in parallel lines fifty feet apart. One person from New York (or Boston) goes across to the opposite side, and walks down the line with her hand outstretched over the outstretched hands of her opponents. When she slaps a hand, the owner immediately tries to catch her before she can reach her side in safety. If the New York (or Boston) person is caught she goes over to her opponents. In either case, the one who chased her becomes the slapper and proceeds on New York's side as the first one had on Boston's side. The object of the game is of course, to catch all one's opponents.

This is My Nose

The leader says, for instance, "This is my nose," but points to her ankle. The one in the group to whom she has pointed must point to her nose and say, "This is my ankle" before the leader counts ten, or she must go down on her knees until a correct answer later reinstates her. The leader continues in similar fashion, pointing to various parts of her body, calling each by the name of some other part. In a large group it is a good plan to have from five to ten people facing the audience, with the leader using them as her "class in mental gymnastics!"

Do This, Do That

The company is put on the floor in gymnastic formation. Orders are given for foolish gymnastic movements, and anyone who obeys a command which is preceded by "Do That" rather than "Do This" must turn his back to the leader. It is a good plan to make this competitive, having the group divided into two sides, and making anyone who makes a mistake drop out. Of course both sides vie for the honor of staying in the game longest.

Magic Music

Send someone out of the room and hide some article on a person with only a small part of it showing. When the searcher returns have everyone sing a popular song.

The nearer he gets to the article the louder the music is, and as he gets farther away the music gets softer. The one on whom the article is found must leave the room next.

The Undesirable Rug

Formation—Double circle in as large a space as possible. At opposite sides of the circle place two rugs or two piles of newspapers. Couples march around until whistle blows unexpectedly. The two couples standing on the rugs or newspapers at the time the whistle blows must drop out of the circle. The rugs are gradually brought in closer as the circle grows smaller. Everyone must walk across the rugs, no one is allowed to side-step or jump.

Side-Step

Formation—Double circle with extra men or girls in the center. Partners stand facing the center, the girl standing in front of the man. That position is called "As you were." For "Back to back" the girl faces center and man faces outside. For "Vis à Vis," partners face.

These positions are called very rapidly and not in any regular order, and everyone is to take them at once. Suddenly the order "Side-step" is given and everyone must get a new partner. Those who don't get partners side-step to the center.

Poison Beanbag

Formation—Circles with not more than fifteen or sixteen in each circle; one in center. A beanbag or a knotted handkerchief is thrown across the circle from one to the other, the one in the center trying to catch it. If he succeeds the one who threw it must change places with him.

Snatch the Handkerchief

The group is divided as for "Smiles." Some object, such as a handkerchief, is put on a small support between each pair of leaders. At a signal, these two come cautiously toward the object, carefully watching each other, each trying to snatch the object and get back to the line without being caught or touched. If touched with the object in hand, a point goes to the other side. They then go to the end of the line, and the new leaders try. Twenty-one is usually the limit.

Puppies Fly

The group may be seated in any formation. The leader says "Robins fly," and raises his arms up and down in a flying motion. The group does the same. This is repeated, using the name of anything that flies. If the leader names something that does not fly, as, for example "Elephants fly" or "Puppies fly," no one should fly. The leader "flies" whether right or not. Anyone who makes a mistake turns his face to the wall.

A Nosy Nose

Six or seven well known people are taken out of a group. A large paper with a hole poked through it is hung in front of the audience. One by one the people behind the scenes poke their noses through the hole, lingering until the audience guesses the owner of the nose. A huge cardboard nose may also be used. Instead of noses, eyes may be shown. In either case, in small groups this may be made into a guessing contest.

The Ridiculous Handkerchief

The leader should be a person with a contagious laugh. He is provided with an ordinary white handkerchief, which, facing the players, he throws into the air. At this signal everybody must laugh as heartily as possible as long as the leader laughs. If anyone continues to laugh after the leader has stopped, he must offer a forfeit.

Postoffice

Group is divided into circles of about fifteen. One player in each circle is blindfolded and is called the postman. Another is postmaster. The remainder of the players are seated. There are no empty chairs. The postmaster assigns each player, including the postman, the name of a city or town, a list of which he keeps. The blindfolded postman is placed in the center of the room and the postmaster takes a position where he can overlook the players. He then calls out, "I have sent a letter from St. Louis to New Haven," and the players representing these cities quickly change places. As they run, the postman tries to capture one of them, and if he can do this or can manage to sit down in an empty chair, the player who is caught and the one whose chair he has taken becomes the postman.

Charades

The company is divided into two groups, each group taking turns at acting out a given word in pantomime.

If the guessing side fails to guess the word being acted out, the other side gets another turn.

Serial charades may be given from week to week by a club or group which meets regularly, the guessers of one charade being given the interim between meetings in which to prepare a charade for the other side.

If a group is very large, two groups made up of five each may be chosen to act out charades. Each group takes turns at acting out a word in pantomime. If the audience guesses the word within three minutes, the side which acted it must give up and each member chooses one from the audience for a new group of five. If the audience fails to guess the word within the required time, the word is given to them and the group has another turn.

Suggested words:

Aeroplane	Air-oh-plane
Antarctic	Aunt-ark-tick
Automobile	Ought-oh-mob-eel
Bandage	Band-age
Bookworm	Book-worm
Broomstick	Broom-stick
Buccaneer	Buck-can-ear
Charlatan	Char-lay-tan
Cribbage	Crib-age
Eyelash	I-lash
Falcon	Fall-con
Forswear	Four-swear
Handicap	Hand-eye-cap
Handkerchief	Hand-cur-chief
Handsome	Hand-some
Holocaust	Hole-oh-cost

Hornpipe	Horn-pipe
Infancy	In-fan-sea
Madcap	Mad-cap
Masquerade	Mass-cur-aid
Melancholy	Melon-collie
Microscope	My-crow-scope
Penitent	Pen-eye-tent
Pilgrimage	Pill-grim-age
Sausage	Saw-sage
Stiletto	Still-let-toe
Truculent	Truck-you-lent
Watchman	Watch-man

Games for Small Groups

The Variegated Chorus

An object is hidden somewhere with only a small part of it showing. The guests are asked to come into the room and search for it. No one is allowed to touch anything, move a curtain or lift a book, since a part of the object is in view. Nor is anyone allowed to talk. As soon as a guest sees the object, he gives no evidence of discovering it, other than to take a chair and start to sing a song. As each one finds the object, he is to continue to hum or whistle or la-la until the last person has discovered it.

Left-Hand Portrait

Each guest is asked to draw the portrait of his left-hand neighbor and put the name of the subject on the back. These are collected and later in the evening are numbered, pinned on a curtain, and guessed. A prize is given to the one who has the most correct answers as to the identity of the portraits.

Number Fortune

Each player is given one or more numbers and a corresponding number of questions. The leader then asks her question, for instance, "Who is the prettiest person in this room?" She now takes up one from a duplicate pack of numbers, which she has on the table. If it is 7, the one having that number must say, "It is I." An assistant who has the names of all of those playing writes opposite No. 7's name "Prettiest." No. 7 now asks his question, "Which one here likes money most?" The leader again takes up a number and reads it. It may be No. 11, who responds, has it recorded against his name and then asks the next question. This is continued until all the numbers are called. At the close of the game each one's record is read. Where players are good friends, questions such as "Who likes fried onions?" "Who is in love?" "Who is very fond of himself?" "Who weighs the most?" may be asked.

Lung Capacity

A line is stretched across the room about seven feet from the floor. At a signal a feather is blown into the air, each side trying to blow it over into the territory of the opposite side. A point is won every time the feather touches the floor or a person. A toy balloon may be used instead.

Soap Bubbles

Soap bubbles may be used instead of feathers or

balloons. The formation is just like that for Lung Capacity. Add a little glycerine to the soapsuds to make the bubbles less likely to break. The sides take turns in making bubbles. No bubble counts until it has once passed over the line. Therefore if it breaks on the way up no score is made. If the bubble blown by A side breaks on B side, it counts one for A. If B blows it back and it breaks on A side, it counts one for B. This continues until each one on both sides has blown a bubble. Score is kept.

Camouflaged Conversation

Group decides on a common adjective, noun or verb, choosing words with more than one meaning, such as "can." The guesser asks question in turn, and the answers should be sentences bringing in the hidden word, but using "teapot" instead of the word. If the word were "can" and the question were "Where is it?" the answer might be, "You teapot find teapots in all teapoteries where they teapot fruit."

Small Talk

The girls in the group are seated so that there is an empty chair between every two girls. The men stand in the center of the room until a signal is given, whereupon they take any seat. Then the men are given cards with topics of conversation written upon them. For example:

1. Suffrage
2. The Bachelor Girl
3. The Next Presidential Election

4. The Ideal Man

5. The Ideal Woman.

The men then begin their first conversation upon the first topic with the girls to their left. This may last for a given time, at the end of which the hostess rings a bell. Anyone heard talking about anything but the assigned topic must sing a song in the center of the room. The men all move to the right and discuss with the next girl the second topic of conversation, and so on until every man has had one conversation with every girl in the room. Then votes are taken secretly by both the men and the girls as to which one has been the best conversationalist. Prizes are awarded to the best man and the best girl conversationalist.

Confusion

One person goes out of the room, but before going he is told that when he comes back he is to ask a question of each person in turn in regard to some object which they shall have chosen during his absence for him to guess. All questions must be such as can be answered by "Yes," "No" or "I don't know." After this player has gone out, the hostess explains to the other players, who are seated around the room, that each is to fix upon his left hand neighbor as the object to be guessed and to answer all questions as they apply to this person. It will be well to arrange the party, so that there will be first a girl, then a man, and so on all around the circle. This makes for complication. A girl, upon being asked "Is it a man?" answers "Yes." The next question might be, "Is he sitting near you?" Answer, "Yes." The questioner can ask only two questions of each person. As he passes on to her neighbor he asks, perhaps, "Is it you?" Answer, "No." Question, "But it is some man in this group, isn't it?" Answer, "No!"

Maidens' Fortune

The girls are given paper and pencils, and are directed to write a list of twenty-three things (given in the first column). These are signed and exchanged for the paper of the neighbor two seats to the right. Then the following questions are asked them in turn and they read the answers as written:

1. Write Yes or No.	Have you a lover?
2. State a gentleman's name.	What is his name?
3. Give a number.	How old is he?
4. Length of time.	How long have you known him?
5. Yes or No.	Does he know you love him?
6. Yes or No.	Is your affection returned?
7. Yes or No.	Has he proposed?
8. A color.	What color is his hair?
9. A color.	What color are his eyes?
10. Yes or No.	Is he handsome?
11. Yes or No.	Is he conceited?
12. Give a number.	How many teeth has he?
13. A color.	What color are they?
14. A shape.	What shape is his nose?
15. A measure.	What size is his mouth?
16. A sum of money.	What is his fortune?
17. A sum of money.	How much will he allow you?

18. A virtue.	What is his chief virtue?
19. A fault.	What is his chief fault?
20. A profession.	What is his profession?
21. The name of a place.	Where did you first meet?
22. A lady's name.	What is your rival's name?
23. The name of a place.	Where do you intend to live?
24. A number.	How many other proposals have you had?
25. Yes or No.	Will the marriage be a happy one?
26. State a time.	When will you be married?

Tell-Tale Proverbs

The leader picks about five or six people asking each one to be prepared with a proverb. When called upon, each one in turn acts out his proverb in pantomime, until the audience guesses it. When the proverb is guessed, each one may choose another person, who in his turn must present a proverb.

Or, each person may tell a story which illustrates his proverb, using all the action necessary to make it dramatic. He, too, may choose someone to illustrate another proverb.

Singing Proverbs

The players are divided into two groups. A proverb is selected, and one word given to a player. If there are more players than words, the same word is given to several people. At a signal from the leader the players of the first group sing their words in concert to a given time. The opposite side must guess the proverb before they can sing theirs.   Proverbs may be shouted instead of sung.

Slang

The players are given pencils and paper and asked to write down all the slang words they can think of in five minutes.   When the time limit is reached the hostess collects the papers and reads the lists of slang expressions.   The players have been previously told that a prize will be given.   When the time comes for its presentation, the hostess gives it to the one who has the shortest list.

Musical Neighbors

Half of the company is blindfolded.   They are then seated so that each has a vacant chair at his right hand. The remaining half of the players now gather in the middle of the room in perfect silence.   At a signal each of the unblindfolded players takes one of the empty seats.   When requested to sing, the unblindfolded ones must do so, disguising their voices as they choose.   The blindfolded persons listen attentively, and each tries to guess who his singing right hand neighbor is.   No blindfolded player is to remove his bandage until he gives correctly the name of his right hand neighbor.

The Crazy-Quilt Story

Cut an exciting short story into paragraphs, mix them up and pass them out to the guests who are sitting in a circle.   Someone is asked to begin the story by reading his paragraph aloud.   When he finishes, his right hand neighbor takes it up, reading his paragraph; then his right hand neighbor in turn reads his, and so on around the circle. A wildly exciting story is the result.

This may be played using only the adjectives in the story. A list is made of all the adjectives and each is written on a separate slip of paper. They are mixed up and given out to the group. The leader begins reading the story, omitting the adjectives for which she asks one in the group in turn. Guests furnish adjectives from the pack dealt out to them.

Progressive Poetry

Each guest is given a sheet of paper and told to write an original line of poetry. He folds over this line and tells his neighbor the last word. The neighbors, knowing only the last word of the previous line, add a second line to rhyme with the first. These in turn are folded over and passed on again for another line, and so on, in each case the neighbor knowing the last word of the preceeding line, so that the poem is a succession of couplets. When the poems have been around the circle each person reads aloud the complete poem that has finally reached him.

Out-of-Door Games

For the smaller out-of-door party, like the kind given on lawns for a group of men and women, a great many of the games given for the indoor programs may be used very successfully. The musical ones especially are most effective. Out-of-door Grand Marches are beautiful, and ''Popularity'' played on a lawn where there is plenty of room to maneuver so as to get the other man's partner has no equal. If an orchestra of two or three pieces is not available, four or five Kazoos can furnish music for even a larger group. They are small pipes through which one sings and the sound of the voice is so magnified that the music carries a long way. They can be purchased at almost any music store for a very small sum.

The old-fashioned singing games, "Farmer in the Dell," "London Bridge," "Old Dan Tucker," "Happy is the Miller Boy," "Captain Jinks," "Skip to Ma Lou, My Darling," have been the most popular of all out-of-door games. Most of these are found in Miss Hofer's book, "Polite and Social Dances."

Couple Tag

All but two men take partners. One of these men is the pursuer and the other the pursued. The pursued man, to save himself, runs and catches the free arm of any girl. She is then his partner and her partner is now pursued until he, too, saves himself by catching a girl for a partner. If he were tagged before he could do this, he, of course, is "It" and becomes pursuer. The game is made very much more exciting if all couples will avoid the pursued man, thus making it far more difficult for him to get a partner.

Tug of War

Two teams. The rope is placed on the ground and the teams, both of which are fifteen yards away, run up, pick up the rope and pull.

The Danger Signal

Two teams, line formation, twenty-five yards apart. Team A marches toward team B until on the blast of the whistle team A turns and runs to its base line pursued by Team B. Team B must not start until the whistle blows. Any whom they touch must go back as prisoners, and the game goes on, the sides taking turns in marching toward opponents. If it is possible, use music and have them march until the music stops.

New Three Deep

This is played like the old "Three Deep," except that the couples stand facing, holding each other's hands. The runner dodges in between them and the one on whom he turns his back must run.

New York

The players are divided into two equal parties, facing each other a short distance apart. One side advances saying, "Here we come," the other side, "Where from?" "New York!" "What's your trade?" "Lemonade!" "Give us some!" Whereupon the first side proceeds to act in pantomime a trade previously decided upon. When the guessing side shouts the correct answer the first side runs back to the goal, and those who are tagged join the opposite side, which then takes its turn at pantomime.

Line Ball

The sides are evenly divided. A line is stretched about seven feet from the floor or ground. The object is to keep the ball, preferably a basketball, from touching the floor. If one side can throw the ball in such a manner that it is not caught but lands on the floor, it scores one point for that side. If the ball touches the line or does not go over, one point is given the opposite side. This game may be closed by either a time limit or a score limit. Any number may play. With a large group, use two or three balls.

Swat Ball

Use volley ball. Divide groups into two teams. Arrange the first team in a straight line at one end of the field; the other in a formation to cover the field. First one in the first team knocks the ball with his fist into the field. If the ball is caught the batter is out, otherwise he runs to the base at the further end of the field and tries to return home without being hit by the ball. Opponents cannot run with the ball but must pass it. After three outs the sides change places. A runner who has run to the given point and back scores one point. He, of course, goes to the end of the line and awaits his turn to bat again.

Scotch Ball

Position as in baseball. Use volley ball. Rules as in baseball, with the following exceptions:

1. Ball is batted by hand (not fist).
2. Runner can be put out by being hit by a thrown ball.

NOTE.—For further Out-of-Door Games see "Games for Either Large or Small Groups" and "Races." See "Games for the Playground, Home, School and Gymnasium," by Jessie H. Bancroft, for directions for Three Deep, etc.

Table Games

"What Would You Do If?"

The following questions and answers are in their right order. Have all the questions typed on one sheet and the answers on another. Cut them apart and, after mixing them up, give each girl on one side a question and on the other an answer. Let the girl at the head of the question side ask her question of the girl at the foot of the answer side, and so on up and down both lines.

What would you do if you had to swim out to Honolulu?

I would put on a bathing suit and dive in.

What would you do if you were given a $25.00 hat?

I would say, "Thank you."

What would you do if the postman brought you a letter containing a check for $1,000.00?

I would give $500.00 to the Red Cross.

What would you do if you were given a ticket to California?

I would pack my grip and start out.

What would you do if you slipped and turned your ankle?

I would go to bed for a week.

What would you do if you had to sing tonight?

I'd sing Yankee Doodle.

What would you do if you fell off the street car?

I would send for a trained nurse.

What would you do if you heard Miss ———— was going to be married?

I would run for a bucket of water.

What would you do if you were introduced to Charlie Chaplin?

I would put it in the paper so everybody would know.

What would you do if you were offered the position of private secretary to the Governor?

I would hire a taxi and take my friends for a ride.

What would you do if you spent your last cent?

I would telephone for the police.

What would you do if you had to live on beans for a week?

I would join the cooking class at the Y. W. C. A.

Mixed Letters

Sets of letters of the alphabet can be bought at any toy store. They are mixed up and put in the center of the table, after each guest has been given four letters to start with. They draw letters one by one in turn, from the center pile, trying always to form a word with their letters. Such words are place in lines before them. If someone is able to form a compound word with the aid of a whole word taken from someone else, he is privileged to take from his neighbor all the letters forming that word. For example, if one guest has the letters s-k-i-n, and a neighbor has s-e-a-l, the first guest may take all the latter's letters. A time limit is set, and a score taken of the number of words formed.

Rapid Roll Call

Each person announces the name of the animal he has chosen, the longer the better. They are all given an equal number of cards (any kind of numbered cards may be used), which are turned face down in a pile, and simultaneously each one takes the top card of his pile and turns it face up, making another pile of face-up cards. If two cards of the same number are turned up, their owners call out each other's animal names. The one who first calls out the other's name is privileged to give him all the cards he has already turned up. The object of the game is to get rid of one's cards.

Eggshell Football

The contents of an egg are blown out. Guests, in two teams, kneel on opposite sides of a table. Object is to blow the egg so that it will fall over the edge of the table on the opponent's side. This scores one point. No one is allowed to touch the egg or the table in any way.

Games of Limited Action

The following games are particularly good where action is limited, as on launch rides or hay-rick rides.

The Fairy Tale

One person begins to tell a story, which is made funnier by bringing in local color. He is given one minute, and at the end of that time his right-hand neighbor takes it up where he left it, continuing the story for another minute, and so on. This may be continued indefinitely until the closing chapter is announced, when each one must give the fate of at least one character.

Traveling Animals

Good for truck or hay-rick ride. The truck or hay-rick is divided roughly into two groups. Each group keeps a sharp look-out on its own side for certain animals. If one side, for example, sees a black cat sitting on a door-step, it counts ten for that side. A yard full of black chickens counts five; a yellow dog, five; a red pig, five; a white horse, ten; a rooster on a fence, ten; a guinea hen, five; a white rabbit, five, etc., etc. A score keeper is appointed for each side, and he calls out each new score as it is reported to him. The game is usualy 500 but it can be abruptly terminated if one side finds a yellow cat in a front window.

Shopping

The first one says, "I've been shopping to-day." Her right hand neighbor asks her, "What did you buy?" and she answers, perhaps, "An egg-beater." "How does it go?" she is asked. "Like this"—and she imitates the action of an egg-beater. Her neighbor, in turn, tells her right-hand neighbor, and so on around the group, each one imitating the action of the thing she bought. After several rounds, this may be changed by limiting the articles bought to objects one can touch, and then again to objects beginning with the initials of one's name.

Mind Reading

The group decides on an object while one person's ears are closed. When the group is ready he begins his questioning by asking which kingdom it is in, animal, mineral or vegetable. Through his questioning, by the process of elimination, he narrows it down, usually guessing the object decided upon in a few minutes. In one case the object decided upon was the last bullet fired by the Germans in the war. It was guessed in one minute and a half.

Gossip

The first player rapidly whispers a sentence to the second, who repeats to the third what he thought it was, and so on until the sentence comes back to the first player who announces the original sentence and the last garbled version!

CHAPTER VII

Games

Baseball on Horseback

Eighteen girls on a team. Each player, who should be small, sits on a "horse" who is on all fours. The diamond is very much smaller than the regular indoor diamond, not more than one-third the regular size. Rules are exactly the same as those of indoor baseball. If a batter makes a hit her horse starts for first base, and then watches her chance to steal second, and so forth. Every play, even to chasing the balls, is made on the horses.

Rubber Hose Baseball

Like indoor baseball, except that there is no pitcher. A piece of hose one foot long lies across two bricks at home plate. Hose is kicked. Rules as in indoor baseball.

Jan Ken Po

This is used a great deal by Oriental children in making decisions as to which team is "up to bat" first, just as we flip a coin. The two leaders shake their closed right hands three times and after the third shake, throw. The first and second fingers extended in a V make scissors; the open hand paper and a closed hand a stone. The scissors can cut the paper; the paper can wrap the stone; and the stone can break the scissors. If, for example, you have thrown "stone" and your opponent has thrown "paper," he wins. If, however, you throw "stone" again and he threw "scissors," you win. The usual two out of three is required.

Girls' Football

The opponents sit in two long rows facing each other. The referee rolls the ball down the middle. The players try to kick the ball over the heads of their opponents, which scores one point. Hands are used as braces behind and must not be used for the ball. A referee is needed at each end to keep the ball within the lines.

The Great Divide

Two lines face each other, separated by a chalk line. The object is to pull individuals across the line, holding by the hands only. This makes them members of the other team.

Snakes and Birds

The group is divided evenly. Those who are snakes are divided into threes and hold hands across the line. At a signal, the others, who are birds, are let out of the cage. The snakes try to encircle them, and if caught, the birds are sent back into the cage until all the birds are caught.

Aesthetic Dancing

The players form a circle standing about two feet

apart from each other. The leader stands in the middle, holding a long stout string, to the end of which is tied a small book wrapped in paper. He whirls this book around the circle, holding it by the string, each time coming nearer the feet of the players who form the circle. The book comes nearer and nearer until the players must jump to avoid being hit. As soon as the book touches the feet of any one, that person must drop out until five people have been put out. Then a new circle is formed, with the first one who had been hit in the center.

Square Tag

The group is divided into two equal lines. They are placed at diagonal corners of a square. Each person has his hands on the shoulders of the one in front of him, and, at a signal, the lines begin to run around the four corners of the square. The leader of each line tries to touch the last one of the other line. Score is kept, and after each point the lines go back to their starting places and begin again. The time limit is four minutes.

Ball Tag

The lines are arranged as in Square Tag. At a signal, the leader of each line begins to run around the square carrying a ball. Each should try to touch the running opponent. Two score-keepers keep score of every one touched. The runners, when they get back to their own lines, hand the ball to the next runner, the first one of the line, and then go to the end of the line.

Take-away

The sides are divided evenly. A basketball is thrown up by the referee. The object is to keep the ball in the hands of your side only, the other side trying to snatch it away. It is against rules to touch any player's body, or to touch the ball when it is in the hands of another.

Tug of War

This may be played in three ways. The formation of the first two is two even lines behind leaders who are facing each other:

1. With hands around waists.
2. Clasping rope.
3. Lines facing, with wrists clasped.

The Dummy

The group is divided evenly into lines. In front of each line is one person with her back turned to the line. Someone in the line hits her with a soft ball (not on head). She must turn around and try to guess who hit her. If she guesses correctly, that girl is the next dummy.

Kick Ball

The group is divided evenly. Each side is divided into two lines, one front, one back, all facing center. A ball is thrown down center. The object is to kick the ball through openings in the back line. The ball must not be touched by hands. The players may follow the ball through the back line.

End Ball

Diagram:

A	B	B	A	A	B
Forward	Guard	Center	Center	Guard	Forward

Centers bat ball back to guards, who try to get it to forwards. Only ball caught on fly counts. Fouls are stepping over lines or walking.

Races

Rope Jump

Relay formation with double lines. The last couple of each group stands about fifteen feet back of the rest of the group. These two carry a short rope between them. At a signal they run forward, carrying the rope over the heads of the others who stoop. When they have reached the front they lower the rope and back up, each couple jumping over the rope. The rope is dropped at the starting point and the running couple moves up to the rear of the group while the front couple immediately runs back, picks up the rope and repeats this. The side which first has its original "rope-bearers" in the starting point wins.

Ball Over Line

Relay formation.—A line is stretched about eight feet from the floor. Leaders are supplied with volley or

basket balls. Each runner must run to the line, throw
the ball over and, going to the other side of the line,
catch it before it touches the ground. The ball must be
caught. A failure to catch it makes it necessary to
throw it over again, repeating this until it is caught.
He then runs back to touch off the next runner.

Team Race

Form teams in columns of threes, fours, or fives, each
one with her hands on the shoulders of the one in
front of her. Teams run about fifty yards, swing from
right to left around some object, race to the starting
point, swing again around the object, make one more
lap and finish across the line.

The Weavers

Have two or three circles in a group competing. One
person from each circle is chosen for starter. He drops
outside the circle, and every one in the circle takes his
neighbors' hands. At a signal the starters from each
circle begin racing, going into the circle under one
pair of arms, and out through the next, in and out
until they reach their own places, where they touch off
the next weaver, the one to the right. The prize goes
to the circle in which the last runner first reaches the
starter.

Shoe Scramble

The contestants line up at one end of the room, race
to the other, take off one shoe and throw it on the pile.
As soon as each one gets her shoe off, she runs back to
the starting line and then on back to the place where the

shoes are piled. There is a wild scramble to find the right shoe, which each contestant must put on and lace up, then racing back to the starting line.

Competitive Leap Frog

Formation—Two circles, described in the following manner. The first girl takes three steps and squats on all fours. The next one hops over her, and each one following does the same thing until the last one has hopped over the first one. The two circles compete as to time.

The combination of "Skin and Snake" (Bancroft) and "Leap Frog" makes a very good gymnasium game.

Relay Races

The principle of relay racing can be used in any number of different races.

1. Running.
2. Jumping, both feet together.
3. Over obstacles.
4. On all fours, first one face down, second one face up.
5. Hop, step and jump. (Stand on one foot and hop, striking on the same foot; second step, step to the opposite foot, and third, jump and land on both feet.)

Wheelbarrow Race

Two girls make a team. One girl of each team stands on the floor on her hands while the other girl holds her feet up as she would the handles of a real wheelbarrow. She guides the human wheelbarrow, who walks on her hands. Teams line up in relay formation and race to a certain point and return, touching off the next team.

Obstacle Race

From four to eight lines of obstacles are laid out for a race for speed. This may be a relay race.

NOTE:—See chapter on Races.

A Foolish Swimming Meet

The following events may be placed on the program of a real Swimming Meet.

1. Tub Races.

2. Tournaments in which each contestant stands in a shaky boat holding a long pole padded at the end, with which she tries to push her opponent into the water.

3. Swimming the length of the pool with a lighted candle in the mouth. If the candle goes out, the swimmer must return to have it lighted again.

4. Boat races with handicaps, such as having one oar, or having to use a pair of big table spoons as oars, or a bandanna handkerchief for a sail.

5. Running races through shallow water.

6. Tugs of War.

7. A tea party with hostess and guests dressed in kimonos, serving and drinking tea as they tread water in deepest water possible, with a floating shingle serving as a tea table.

8. Egg Balance. Each contestant carries a spoon in her mouth and balances an egg in the spoon.

Indoor Track Meet

Have the colors of four colleges made of cheese cloth or ribbon and pin one to each girl as she enters. When ready for the events, the representatives of each college take their places under their banners in a corner of the room or gymnasium. If it is to be a big event, the songs and yells may have been learned in advance. A manager with a megaphone calls out the events, and an equal number of representatives from each college come to the center of the floor and compete. The events may be varied according to the occasion. There may be some real jumping, running, etc., interspersed with mock events, or they may be all of either kind. Points for first and second place may be given.

There may be refreshments in keeping, such as:

Dumb-bells	Pickles
Parallel bars	Straws
Traveling rings	Doughnuts
Baseballs	Round white candy

The nature of the refreshments may be kept secret, and each may be allowed to choose two or three things from a menu posted in front of the serving window. These things may be served on small paper plates. Later another surprise of something more substantial may be given to all.

The medals, cups, etc., may be given out during the time for refreshments. Round tins may be used for medals, with a safety pin fastened through a hole in the center. These may be given to individual winners. A loving cup may be made from two funnels, one a little smaller than the other. A tinner can take off the ends and solder them together, adding handles if desired. This may be given to the winning college, with an inscription written on it.

Following is a suggested program:

(Unless otherwise stated, it is well to have just one contestant from each group to enter each event.)

Bawl Game

Let the judges decide who can "bawl" the best.

Hurdle Race

Sing "America," singing two words, omitting two words, etc. A mistake puts one out.

The Bone of Contention

Two girls face each other, sitting on the floor. Their feet are braced up together and must remain so. Their knees must remain straight. Together they grasp a bar or a broomstick handle and at a signal try slowly to pull each other to a standing position. It usually results in one of them falling headlong over the other.

Johnny Jump Up

Each group gets into line. The first one of each group jumps as far as possible, marking at heel. The next one starts at chalk line and continues. Side reaching farthest point wins.

Wide Stretch

Each group gets into line. Every one in four different lines stretches arms out shoulder high, touching finger tips. Longest line wins.

Hanker Throw

Throw a handkerchief as far as possible with no weight or knot.

Feather Blow

Each one is given a feather, and at a signal blows it high in the air. The object is to keep the feathers in the air the longest possible time.

Scent Push

The participants race to shove pennies across a sheet by pushing them with their noses.

Running High Squeal

Each contestant runs a short defined distance and squeals. The one squealing highest, scores.

Pot Shoot

Set a mason jar on the floor. Each girl has six beans. Hold at arm's length and drop into jar.

Yard Measure

Draw lines on a blackboard a yard long, by guess.

Bag-Leg

Race with legs in a bag.

Pole Vault

A race to eat bars of candy.

Blow Bags

Common paper sacks are blown up and contestants throw for distances.

Vocal High Jump

Contestants say one word high and one word low with their faces straight.

Yard Dash

Push pennies along yard sticks with tooth picks.

Cripple Race

Two in a team race with inside ankles tied together.

Laughing Contest

Points are given for the following events:
1. Variations of a laugh.
2. Continuity of a laugh.
3. Most changeable laugh.

Standing High Jump

Four doughnuts are suspended in a doorway, about four inches above the mouths of the jumpers. The contestants eat their doughnuts with hands tied, with speed in finishing as the object of the race.

Gloomy Gus

Two girls are chosen from each group. Four of them, of different groups, are to try to keep solemn, in spite of everything the other four do.

NOTE:—In addition to these events, see chapter on Races as well as those given in this chapter.

THE ICE-BREAKER
HERSELF

Practical Suggestions
for
Recreation Leadership

THIS BOOK IS DEDICATED

TO

MERLE HUFF

THE ICE-BREAKER
HERSELF

THE ICE-BREAKER HERSELF

Recreation Leadership

"Say! Do you get paid for doing this? Anybody who had as much fun as you had to-night ought to pay an admission fee rather than get a salary for it!"

A soldier said this to me after a large party for soldiers and girls which I had put on in a cantonment city. I was set up. If I had given the impression that my decidedly strenuous work for the past three hours was such keen enjoyment to me that I was indebted to my guests, perhaps I was on the way to becoming a real recreation leader!

I had really enjoyed every minute of that party and had laughed until the tears came. But the same remark could not have been made after my first appearance as recreation leader for a large crowd. I went home a nervous wreck and vowed I'd never put on another party as long as I lived.

I know why, now; it was because I was there as a distinct individual; I was there to "entertain" those guests, to teach them games, and I did and was all the things I shouldn't have done and been!

Perhaps you, who are so discouraged over your social evenings, are making some of my mistakes. But before we begin, let's understand this. Just as soon as we've

learned all the rules of recreation leadership, just as soon
as we get cocksure that we can do it because we know
how, just then is when we'll begin to backslide! There
is no such thing as perfect recreation leadership. Every
time a leader, a real leader, meets a group she discards
some of her choicest hard and fast rules and regulations,
and installs new ones in their place!

And at that, it is not knowing rules and regulations
that makes one a recreation leader. The first big essential to leadership is the right attitude of mind.

Attitude

In recreation leadership you, as an individual, are not
present; your self is not anywhere around. You are pri-
marily a medium through which something in which you
have implicit faith must get over to your guests.

The finest compliment ever paid me came at the hard-
est party I have had to put on. Hundreds of soldiers
and girls were there as guests, and as an audience there
was a most critical group of officials. When the party
was all over, the greatest of the critical dignitaries came
to me and said, "Do you know that I never once was
conscious that you were within a hundred miles of this
place? I was so fascinated by watching those men and
girls that I didn't know you were about!"

And I wasn't there. I was so intent on getting over
this big thing to those men and girls, that anything
might have happened to me and I wouldn't have known
it. Not one thing personal except personality can matter. For example there is the awful inevitable feeling of
stage-fright. There isn't one of us who hasn't felt it,
and experienced that almost overwhelming desire to run

away. You, as an individual, have a perfect right to run, but you as a recreation leader have no right to yield to such personal things as fear, stage-fright and that overwhelming sense of responsibility. You as a private individual with all the rights of a private individual, do not exist. It is only as a medium that you have a right to be directing. But each time you conquer any personal feeling of weakness you gain new strength and immunity against such diseases.

Does it seem to you that as a medium you necessarily lose personality? Never have you needed personality more, and never was a better chance given you to use your own distinct personality. It is evident in every direction you give and in every word you speak. More than that, through every direction, through every word, through your posture, your voice, your eyes, you proclaim either that this business of leading is a painful duty which must be performed, or that it is a real joy and an ever-increasing one.

Leading recreation cannot be that joy, however, until you look upon recreation as more than "games." You must look upon recreation as a real force with tremendous possibilities for bringing out the very best in a person; with possibilities that enable one to interpret life and to live life joyfully; possibilities for turning leisure time into an asset rather than a liability; for sustaining happy, normal life. There are so many possibilities in recreation. If you do have faith in recreation as being re-creation, and if you can lose yourself in so interpreting it, then your task of leadership must inevitably be a joyful one.

Does that sound impossible? If you yourself are once thoroughly convinced, then your attitude is inevitably and unconsciously that you are there not to teach games, but rather to share with your guests something wonderful and joyful. And because joy is contagious, I leave to you what happens!

But to make recreation contagious a recreation leader must (with heavy underlining for the "must") be at ease, at least ostensibly so. We are working for relaxation. How can we expect our guests to relax and really recreate when we as leaders are very plainly so scared and so tense and so nervous about things going right that the very atmosphere is nervous? It hardly seems necessary to say that unless the leader is at ease there is no possible chance that her guests will feel so.

Are you saying that it is impossible for the beginner to feel at ease, though it might be easy enough for the person born with the gift of recreation leadership? Remember that I said "ostensibly at ease." You cannot show me a veteran recreation leader who will not admit that before some parties she cannot eat a bite of dinner from sheer nervousness. Yet she will stand up before her group that night and look as though all this were a mere detail in her busy life and she will have as much fun as anyone there. No one gave her that accomplishment! She has had to work very consciously toward that goal. She knows that ease is essential to the spirit of relaxation. She knows too that a thing well-done looks easy. That is why she has put forth every effort to master the technical details of her work so that she may be absolutely free for the bigger thing,—which is to create the spirit of re-creation.

We say that a leader must be at ease and yet full of life and energy and enthusiasm. In the effort to appear at ease I have seen leaders take on a bored air, but a disinterested leader never gets a thing across. On the other hand, neither does a noisy, disorganized "peppy" leader. How I do dislike that word "pep" which so many people think essential to recreation leadership! It always makes me think of something gone wild. The master orchestra leader would make an ideal recreation leader in his quiet, yet perfect and complete control. The more ostentatious "pep" is, the less there is of real recreation. Rather. there is a noisy substitute for it. But enthusiasm is an entirely different thing, enthusiasm that shows in one's eyes, one's bearing, one's whole attitude. Well directed and intelligent enthusiasm is without question the most valuable asset a recreation leader can have, and that kind of enthusiasm comes from an unbounded faith in recreation, a faith that can survive all the bumps and knocks that recreation leaders inevitably get. That kind of enthusiasm is the thing that will successfully get across the gospel of recreation any and every where, any and every time.

Control

The term "Recreation Director" is misleading. Any director who is a director, rather than a leader, has no place in recreation.

Because leaders must first and last have absolute control over their groups, some of them think that directing is necessary to show the group that they are in charge. The finest control possible is that in which no real control is evident, and in which the leader has created so fine and alive an atmosphere that the question of control does not exist. Such a power of control does not come at once. But if a leader conscientiously works toward a leadership in which there is a very real alertness, a sensitiveness to the constantly changing atmosphere, and a sharp lookout for the danger signals which show tendencies toward boisterousness, boredom, or any of the evils that make a party a failure, rather than leadership without any evidence of real assertive control and a leadership in which one's whole personality and the best of one's technique is exerted, then that fine and live atmosphere of which we speak is an inevitable result.

Control, I have learned, is a state of mind. When I began teaching school (fifth grade it was, and *such* a fifth grade!), I could not "make them mind!" Each day was a horror to me. My principal told me over and over that the reason for the lack of discipline was without question my attitude of mind. I just could not see it until it came to me one day with a shock that I was miserably afraid of those children; that I expected things to go wrong, and so they did; that discipline was uppermost in my mind, and because of that I never let myself go, never really lost myself in the thing I was teaching. I found my way out through baseball. I went down to find out what was the trouble and discovered that it was a question as to whether "a guy should run for first base after his third strike." I happened to know and I couldn't resist begging for just one bat. They granted it to me, and luck was with me. I made a home run!

Discipline never entered my head after that. It was not because the boys thought I was a "good sport," but it was because I went at geography in the same way in which I went at baseball, with my heart and soul, and naturally it became the most interesting thing of the moment. With the consciousness of a growing sense of leadership in geography, came a sense of control, if one wishes to call it that, and I discovered that control is one's attitude of mind. Let a leader put her whole personality and thought and enthusiasm into geography or recreation and not on keeping discipline, and discipline is kept.

We hear so much of those boys who come in "just to start something" at church and community parties. If more of the leader's energy and thought were put on making her program intensely interesting and less on keeping discipline, less disciplining would be necessary.

I certainly am not trying to minimize the importance of the leader's having complete control. That is absolutely essential. But she will be far more likely to develop that control if her every thought is put on re-creation and not on "making them mind."

However, situations arise, as situations will. I saw a rare one handled by a leader in a superb way. Two half-intoxicated men came into a community party for the sole purpose of starting something. They began uproariously. What would you have done? Almost invariably the answer is, "I should have asked some of the men to put them out." Do you know what would have happened? Frankly, a fight. That could have been taken care of, but it would have absolutely killed the spirit of play which you had so carefully been fostering. Their being allowed to remain there in that condition would have had the same effect. So would any argument with them.

Those men had to be taken out immediately. We could not afford to jeopardize the splendid spirit of the crowd either by allowing them to stay or by openly putting them out. There were only two entrances to this hall.

Three or four aides were quietly sent to the rear door. The front door had a spring lock on it. "Merry-go-round" was going full swing.

"Won't you help me bring up the ice-cream freezers?" smilingly asked the leader of these two men.

"Why sure, Sweetie. We'd do anything for you," came the answer, together with a great deal more that made the leader grit her teeth, but she kept her smile with her till she got them safely through the front door with the spring latch set. What she did then is beside the point. The real point is that these men who were objectionable in every way were disposed of and not one of the guests knew a thing about it. That was real leadership. "The finest kind of control is where no control is evident."

It is the same principle that takes care of a mischievous Sunday School pupil's energy at a church social, without a definite, "Now, Johnny, if you trip Billy again you can't play." I know that you are thinking that it is easy enough for me to tell you at this point to make the games so interesting that he will not want to get into mischief. I'm not going to tell you that. You ought to know that anyhow. But one thing I am going to tell you as a rockbound truth. You teach "Merry-go-round" in the *right* way, with your heart and soul in the teaching and in the game, and the result is a spirit that makes Johnny say, "Oh, Boy! Let's do that again!" rather than "I wonder if I can start something and get that leader going!" And one last secret— Johnny will find out very quicky whether he *can* "get that leader going!"

As a postscript to these words on control, just a word to the wise about being bossy, either in attitude or in voice. Have you seen leaders with wonderful possibilities fail utterly because of a certain antagonism they aroused? I never shall forget the first party for which I was responsible. I was thoroughly scared both of myself and of the guests, and yet was determined that things must go exactly according to plan. Because a group reflects immediately the attitude of the leader, things at first were horribly stiff and then I began to feel an antagonistic response to what one man called "that bossy leader." Partly to conceal my nervousness and partly to make things go efficiently, and to be sure I had the group in control, I put on a very bossy front, with painful results!

A group of people out for a good time will not be bossed unless there is a huge laugh behind it all. I have seen a fine leader harangue a group of men with no mercy. Did they rise up and smite her? They did not. They laughed until the tears came, partly because of the nature of the criticism (one whole row of men had feet that *would* not track!) but more because behind the words, "You men couldn't do that any worse if you practiced," was a big hearty laugh and a spirit of the best possible kind of good fellowship and friendliness. How did they know? Don't you ever believe that a group does not know. You cannot camouflage. If you feel good fellowship toward your group it will be evident in every word you say, and if you feel bossy, your every move will be bossy.

Getting Attention

Was your first party anything like my first party? Stragglers sat on the sidelines; the couples one by one drifted off by themselves; people talked and buzzed while I shouted in my attempts to make my directions heard. Did your guests, too, get a bit confused and wonder what it was all about? Did they have a 100 per cent good time?

Can you imagine instead a party where every man, woman and child in the room paid the closest attention to every word the leader spoke because to miss a direction would mean to miss the keenest fun one could imagine? Can you see this leader having such an understanding of her group and the elementary psychological principles underlying its actions that she could create hearty laughs merely by the nonsense in her directions?

For example she might want four men for a race. Shall she ask for four men to volunteer? She is missing a wonderful opportunity if she does. Instead she might ask to have the four best-looking men to step forward. Do they step? They do not! Instead she chooses, and in doing it uses good psychology. She chooses a deacon from the Baptist Church, and his colleagues are convulsed; she chooses the principal of the High School who is anything but beautiful; she chooses the shyest man she can find; and then probably "that man who is hiding behind the post." Can you hear the uproar? And because she is a leader she is able to check that hilarity the minute it turns from spontaneous laughter into boisterous racket. Wouldn't it have been too bad for the guests to miss all that fun just because the leader was afraid to drop orthodox technical methods of choosing participants and directing her games?

All of which goes to show that directions should not be just directions. The fun should start the minute you begin to explain a game, not after the game itself is in full swing. Hard work? Not at all. Take "Merry-go-round," our old stand-by. Show them how to do the steps and let them practice. Pick out some man whose spirit you can count on and make all manner of good-natured fun of the way he hops! Again, do not tell them which foot to put to the side first and you will have the funniest imaginable snarl. Or in "I See a Ghost," choose a man to stand next to you who you are sure will get the directions all mixed up. His mistakes in carrying out directions are infinitely funnier than is the game itself. Let the fun start when you start to give directions. So many leaders fall down at this point. They teach a game, and how people do hate to be taught! And how quickly they will drop out of a circle and "just watch this time!" Interest has been allowed to lag because the leader used just directions.

Voice plays as important a part in all of this. Say something right now, and say it in as commonplace a way as you can. Now say it in a bossy way. Now say it as though you were the chairman of the social committee who is going to make "all these dear brothers and sisters have a nice happy time together!" And now say it with the spirit of, "Say! If you people knew what I'm going to do to you right now!" What is in that last voice that makes a group of any size or color or disposition sit up and take notice and not let one word go by? It is personality plus; fun galore; a great big laugh that is with, and not at the crowd; mystery which brings forth a wonder as to what that leader is going to do next; in short, good fellowship in abundance. That last voice is natural; it is you. That is what makes recreation leadership, and that is what will make a crowd listen the minute you begin to talk.

One rule I always observe, never talk down the chatterers in a group. If public opinion does not hush them; if directions are not interesting enough to get their attention; if significant pauses are not successful, stop entirely rather than shout to drown them out. A leader's whole force, physical and mental, is needed in a task so much more worth-while, that it never pays repeatedly to talk down the chatterers. Some one on the sidelines, two people in the fourth row; or some girls in the rear buzzing constantly while you are giving directions, can take a great deal not only from your strength but from the big spirit that you have created—the spirit of one-ness and good healthy fun. If you have "buzzers" it is far more effective to talk in an even tone, hardly raising your voice at all, perhaps saying the same thing over and over until the entire group strains its ears to catch what you are saying, rather than to demand attention by shouting. The first time you shout it is easy to make them stop talking; the next time it is a bit harder, and it grows harder and harder until finally they pay no attention whatsoever to your shouting. On the other hand, the first time you try talking in an even tone it is mighty hard to get attention, but each succeeding time it becomes easier.

Even so, having gained the attention of the group it is sometimes hard to make every one hear. It has proved to be easier to talk to a point just above the heads of those in the rear. If one talks into the crowd, one's voice is lost there. Sometimes a very small megaphone is effective, but use this only with a large crowd, for the voice loses all personality through a megaphone and only words, directions, get to the guests. Use the whistle if it is necessary, but do not overdo it, for it is irritating to have a whistle tooting constantly. One whistle, then perhaps a sibilant "Sh!" from some of your helpers, and you have them.

Directions

Isn't it an all-gone feeling to forget how a game should run? With your group in front of you, waiting, and only too surely conscious of the fact that you have forgotten! Does it give them any more confidence in your power of leadership? Worse still, does it make them any more enthusiastic over play in general? You know we really are having to teach people to play, for so many of us have forgotten how, and it is a tragedy on the part of the leader, because of technical errors and omissions, to do anything to hinder the growing spirit of play in our American grown-ups. If a leader does not have absolute confidence in her ability to teach the technical part of a game, and does not carry that conviction across to her group, how can she expect to swing that much bigger and more intangible thing, the spirit of the game? That is why directions for games should be so completely mastered that they become only a minor issue, and all one's energy and personality can be devoted to creating the spirit that makes a game re-creation. But if at first you cannot be sure that you can remember all directions for all games, use mechanical aids. For example, small cards with a brief outline of new games can be carried in the hand, and will help immeasurably.

In all directions for all games, use the simplest terms and as few terms as possible. Do not overdirect. It is only confusing and detracts from, rather than adds to, the fun of the game. Nor is it at all a new thing for a leader to have scattered through the group a few volunteers who know the principles of the different new games she is going to teach. It makes the work ever so much easier, especially in a game such as the "Virginia Reel." Every one plays that in a different way and if in each set you can have some one who knows your way of teaching it, you will have no trouble at all in swinging a huge group through the different figures with the maximum of enjoyment and the minimum of difficulty.

The Leader's Part in a Game

We have been speaking of the necessity for the leader to be so thoroughly sure of the directions for a game that all her thought can be put on swinging the spirit of the game. Two questions arise out of that. One question comes to me always whenever a group of recreation leaders get together. "Should a leader take an actual part in the game?" If the group is a fairly large one of fifty guests or more, I should say decidedly not. The leader is responsible for the spirit of the entire room, for everything that goes on in the room, and while in her leadership and in her reactions, she may be playing every move of the game herself, her physical self is most emphatically on the outside of the circle.

The second question is, "To what extent does a leader control the actual sport in a game?" In a game like "Merry-go-round," the music absolutely controls the fun in the game and can make or break it, and the leader's part, as far as laughs are concerned, is negligible. But such games are an exception. In "The Undesirable Rug" it is the leader who blows the whistle which catches some unfortunate on the rug. Let her turn her back and try blowing the whistle and immediately the game becomes flat. The whole fun of that game depends on the leader's alertness to ridiculous possibilities and unexpected developments.

The object of this last discussion surely is not to show leaders that in some games one can sit back and let the game take care of itself. Hardly! It is rather to show that giving directions for a game is not enough, and that every development of it must be watched and carefully fostered.

Mistakes

Have you too an awkward member in your group who just never can get directions right and who does everything wrong? And does it irritate you, or do you capitalize those mistakes and get every one to laughing *with* the awkward brother rather than *at* him? There is no surer way to create the finest possible spirit, not only of fun, but of good fellowship. A leader of the social life in a large Middle West church loses much because she insists that every grand march figure be performed perfectly, that every direction be followed implicitly, that mistakes in games be painstakingly corrected. But mistakes are worth noticing only when they interfere with the pleasure of other guests. Instead of correcting why not capitalize or anticipate mistakes? To capitalize them one does not mean to make fun of the one who made a mistake. Laugh with him rather than at him, and you will often find that a mistake in a game will make it infinitely funnier than the original game. Play up to it. If a leader has created the right atmosphere, every one of a set doing the Virginia Reel can be convulsed at the blind struggling efforts of Mr. Jones, who is himself laughing so hard that there is no hope of his getting through the figures. What difference does it make? One hearty spontaneous laugh is worth one hundred correct figures.

But sometimes a mistake will spoil a game. In one grand march figure, for example, if one person makes a certain mistake it confuses the entire group. Sometimes it is hopelessly ruined. Too bad, but why do it all over again just to get it right? Do we go to parties to add to our repertoire of beautifully learned games? But the next time, remember the mistake that was made and anticipate it, and tell them that any one who does not count eight between every figure will probably be stood in the corner for the rest of the evening!

As far as possible, then, anticipate rather than correct mistakes. It is in the reaction, not in the rules, that we are interested; in the player, not in the play.

How Long to Play a Game

The answer to that question is different for every leader, for every group, for every game. When put to a group the answers vary. Some say, "Until you see the interest lagging"; others, "Just before the interest lags"; and others, "When you've been able to make every one laugh."

I should never make so broad a statement. Each game must be studied by itself. If you believe in re-creation rather than in just games, the possibilities in a game for good and bad should be carefully taken into account, and a goal set for that particular game. For example, in "Merry-go-round," while it is invaluable up to a certain point, it would if allowed to go one step beyond a certain limit become decidedly rough and tumble. "This Is My Nose" ceases to be funny and becomes a bore when the participants begin to execute your commands correctly.

Every game we play has a definite purpose and a definite place in our plan for recreation. Some of them exist only to make people laugh and laugh until utter relaxation is inevitable; some combine rhythm with a hearty laugh, than which there is no more healthful or delightful combination; some serve as ice-breakers in a stiff group; some games help eighteen-year-old John appreciate the fact that grandfather is the best sport ever! Each one of them has a definite purpose and each a definite goal. Sometimes the goal is not reached and it is strategic to cut activities off short; sometimes it is wise to go far beyond the set goal, but always it is absolutely essential that the leader watch closely all developments if she would get the best possible out of that game.

Should a Large Group Be Divided?

Can you imagine a party where a fascinating game is going on in the northeast corner, not so lively a game in the southwest corner, a fairly interesting game in the northwest corner, and a really uninteresting game in the southeast corner? Where would all eyes be centered, and what would happen in a few moments?

Suppose that there are too many guests to be directed in a game at any one time by the amateur leader. Can you see that leader putting all men between seventy and thirty-five into a "Lobster Race" down the center of the room? Next, all the red-heads form a small circle in the center and play "Ditto." If you have never seen ten or twelve people playing "Ditto" with a leader who had previously planned diabolical movements to be imitated, you cannot appreciate this! Then fifty-two from the right side of the room play "Alphabet," while all the others act as judges, etc., etc. True, it does take all the strength that a leader has to keep the interest at such a high pitch that guests are content sometimes to be onlookers, but there is so much to be gained from having the entire group together in a unity of feeling, or purpose, of interest, that it is more than worth the tremendous effort needed.

Resting Between Games

To make your guests too tired is to make them a bit irritable and to lessen the enjoyment of an evening. Games like "We Won't Go Home Until Morning" leave one decidedly breathless. A rest is necessary between strenuous games.

But a rest does not necessarily mean inaction. When the guests are sitting still and resting it does not mean that the interest which a leader has consciously worked up to a certain point is allowed to slump, so that when games are started again the leader will have to begin all over. Further plan to have something so interesting going on in the middle of the room during the rest interval that the fire escape has no attractions. Before he knows it, every guest is back on the floor again, rested, yes, but with his interest keener than ever and without the need of further convincing that games are great fun!

For example, can you imagine yourself bored to tears

and wondering how much longer this stupid party is to
last if you were watching two men, seated in chairs in
the middle of the room, each supplied with a baby's
bottle full of milk and the necessary apparatus on top,
drinking the milk in the time-honored manner to see
which can empty his bottle first? Since it is a forgotten
art with both men, there are bound to be complications.
There could hardly be a doubt of sustained interest on
the part of the watching group!

Sustained interest is absolutely essential. There is
plenty of available material which calls for only two or
three participants, and which is fascinating enough to
hold easily the interest of a large group as they rest from
strenuous activity.

Music

Sometimes I think that good music is half the battle.
There is something so fascinating about swinging down
a room eight abreast in a grand march, something that
so gets under your skin that you can not help relaxing
and letting recreation get in its good work. But we
have not space to talk about the value of music, and of
rhythmical games in recreation. To speak particularly
of the technical end of it, your music surely can make
or mar your rhythmical games. I have seen "Noriu
Miego," one of the finest musical games I know for
breaking down the last barrier, become a stiff folk-dance
because the pianist played it with technical perfection
as her only aim. Your music must *talk;* it must get
over the gospel of recreation to all unbelievers; it must
feel all the joy and enthusiasm that we want every one
to feel; it must tell the story to every guest. I know

that it is hard to get that kind of music, but it is worth making every effort to get, for the right kind of music can work wonders, and the wrong kind, havoc!

Have you ever been elegant enough to have a real orchestra furnish music for your grand march and musical games and then have those games turn out to be absolute failures? A piano and a drum have proved the most satisfactory music I have ever had. The low steady rhythm of the drum carries a group along without detracting from the big business of the game, fun, as any louder or shriller instruments invariably do. Nothing is more contagious than laughter, and loud or shrill music always drowns out the sound of laughter, which is one of the most valuable forces you have working for you.

Out-of-door music always seemed so hard to provide, for I've never yet found guests who could or would sing and "Skip to my Lou" at the same time satisfactorily. It leaves one so breathless that there is no strength left for fun. Kazoos easily furnish enough music for even large groups out-of-doors. They can be bought at any ten cent store and can be successfully operated by the least musical person.

Stragglers

In every group there are some little rocks who just want to "set." Of course we urge them to come into the games, but too much urging has a bad effect on them and on others, to say nothing of the wear and tear on you. It is because of those stragglers that we plan to have some big simple movement like the continuous receiving line, at the beginning of the party. This game, in which every one gets into line, men in one and girls in another, seldom fails to get every last one on his feet, for the most bashful man on earth can stand in company with every other man present, and not be paralyzed with fear. This makes the girl who thinks of games as something for children, too conspicuous for her own comfort, as she sits alone when every one else is in the receiving line shaking hands with every other guest. Before they have a chance to drop out we put on some grand march figure which has a big laugh in it, and—recreation is working!

But, you say, they have to be teased all evening every time a new game is started. That is your fault, and my fault, if after giving them a taste of what recreation can be we do not make our programs live enough to hold and increase their interest. For arousing initial interest where at first there was perhaps antagonism to games or shyness or a desire to "be shown," nothing is more successful than the grand march, in which the individual is submerged, and rhythm plus sociability turns the trick.

Which reminds me, at the risk of repeating, what was said under "Gaining Attention," I want to say just a word here about the principle of choosing victims for some events, for, strange as it may seem, it is often through this method that these stragglers are won.

When you want three or four victims for a hoax do you ask for volunteers? They do not come easily, or if they do, they are the same ones every time. Neither is it always successful to pick certain individuals and ask them to step out. If instead you may ask for the best-looking man present to come forward you will either get a very hearty response, which will give you the chance to pick the required number from those who volunteered, or they will all assume great modesty and no one will offer himself. In that case you announce that you will pick the best-looking man present and you may be sure that public opinion will be with you and will force your Apollo to the front because of the big laugh in the whole proceeding! But you do not have the support of public opinion when you merely ask an individual to become a victim, without creating a certain atmosphere. They are all rather sorry for him instead.

Partners

Can it be that in your community as well as in mine certain young people persist in playing with certain other young people and only with them, all through the evening at every party they attend? Do you take them aside after the party and labor with them or do you get a laugh out of the situation which leaves every one with a comfortable feeling?

Perhaps John and Mary insist on being partners all evening. Nothing can separate them. They happen to be third in the line of march. Just as the music begins send James and Billy, who are the first and second in line on an errand; ask the rest of the men to step up two places to fill the vacancies and without waiting a second start your grand march. Mary is still number three, John is leading!

Perhaps if you said, "Every man take a partner," some girls would always be chosen, and some never. There may be a decidedly uneven number of men and girls. Again the answer is the grand march. Have them line up in any fashion, men in one line, girls in the other; the two lines separate, men going one way, girls the other, meeting at the back of the room and coming up the center with partners. At the end of the line, if there are more girls than men, girls take girls for partners, or vice versa.

Can Certain Games Be Played Over?

The revised version of "Musical Chairs" can be used at each one of a series of parties. There is an ever-changing human element in it. The movements in "Merry-go-round" are practically the same each time, but perhaps it could not be used so regularly except for the big irresistible swing of the Merry-go-round that, used in moderation, makes it always a favorite game. I should not repeat such a game as "This Is My Nose" very often, for its novelty lies in the mistakes the players make before they grasp the idea. "The Alphabet Game" is different each time it is played. If the leader prepares her list of words thoughtfully there is no limit to its resources. Competition is at its height in a game like this, and there is an interest that only increases throughout the game. "Magic Music" loses its charm with much repetition because of the limited number of the kind of hiding places which allow the searcher to stare right at the desired object and not see it, while the rest of the group is shrieking out the music which tells him he is warm!

In using games over and over, the leader should know what is the successful element in a game. She should decide whether it is due to novelty, to rhythm, to un-expected changes, or to chance, and govern repetition accordingly.

Formations for Games

We have said, "Let the fun start as soon as you begin giving directions for a game." The grand march helps wonderfully to do that.

You have heard leaders call out, "Take your partners for the Virginia Reel!" If it is a typically up-to-date crowd, you know how they do it and how very quickly they form sets while the leader stands by, cool, calm, and collected! At that, one-half the group sits on the side-lines. Why, then, shall we not fall back on our friend, the grand march? It takes almost no time to get the entire company into a double line, and then the leader goes rapidly down the line counting off by six couples, sending each set to an assigned place, and the game is on.

Perhaps you want sets of four to form a hollow square. It would take too long to get them into position by picking out fours here and there, or to let them do it for themselves. Instead, use the grand march to get guests into line, four abreast. The one at the right end of each line counts for his line, lines counting off by twos. When all lines are numbered, lines numbered one step to left side of room, lines numbered two to right side, the four making up each line joining hands to make a hollow square.

We have found the grand march invaluable in arranging any kind of formation, in that it does it in a very short time with very few directions (that alone makes it worth its weight in gold), and there is fun in it from start to finish. And just between us, people never know what's going to happen to them, and you know the value of that!

There is another important side to this matter of getting people into position for a game and that is the necessity for being careful that no situation shall be created which would make it possible for any one to feel left out or embarrassed.

Perhaps there are a great many more girls than men, and you want a double circle with extra girls inside who will be given a chance to get partners away from their more fortunate sisters. Guests are all seated about the room. The leader ask all men to come to the center of the room. Girls are asked to make a circle around them. Men are asked to choose partners, all extra girls going to the center. Any fun in it? No, only a certain embarrassment on the part of the girls who were not chosen. Instead, "All girls come to the center of the room. Men make a circle around them. At a signal all girls (who can!) get a partner, those who are unsuccessful going back to the center." Result? A rush for a partner, wild excitement, keen competition and a healthy hearty laugh at the girls who were too slow, not too un-beautiful, to get a partner!

Always play up to that element of competition which will make a game even out of directions for a game, as well as leaving no chance for hurt feelings.

A Constructive Program

Always I hear the cry, "But we can't find new games!"

When you look for new games do you pick out games that will do for to-night's party? Next time you want material for a party do you do the same thing? You will never enlarge your repertoire; you will miss endless opportunities for adaptation and revision; and your recreation programs will inevitably be hit or miss. If you know that you have a series of parties for which you will be responsible, try instead going through one book of games from cover to cover and classifying the events and games according to what you consider are your individual needs. That is much easier than it sounds.

The following classification has been found to serve splendidly in the majority of cases:

1.	Small group games.	8.	Races and relays.
2.	Large group games.	9.	Mixing games.
3.	Either large or small group games	10.	To find partners.
		11.	Fortunes.
4.	Table games.	12.	Forfeits.
5.	Limited action games, (such as games for hay-rick rides).	13.	Tricks.
		14.	Stunts.
		15.	Refreshments.
6.	Musical games.	16.	Special parties.
7.	Out-of-doors games.		

It is easy to add new games and ideas to this classification constantly. You will find very soon that a game will classify itself the minute it is suggested to you, and in a very short time you will have a real repertoire of recreation material from which to draw in making a really constructive program.

With this as a basis it is almost inevitable that the next step in planning a series of parties will be to plan the sort of program in which each party is built on the program that preceded it, using its successes as a foundation on which to build and its failures as guide-posts. With that process will come new goals and new ideals, all of which make for an ever-increasing growth in the value and worth-whileness of the recreation you are giving to your community.

Adapting Games

Have you ever asked a group of up-and-coming young people if they would like to play "Going to Jerusalem" or "Musical Chairs"? Perhaps they have played it once and enjoyed it thoroughly, but to use it again brings out, "Oh, that's such an old game!" But it can be made a new game, right up to the latest mark and requirements by bringing in a new, and in this case, human, element. Substitute, for chairs, girls who stand in a single line with right arms crooked. Will your young people call it "old stuff?" No, because of the ever-changing element and the big game of chance in it. That is just one illustration of an adaptation of old material to new requirements.

Choice of Games

We used to say that the most simple games were by far the most successful. We still say that, but more and more we are shifting the burden of responsibility over to the leader. The most successful game is the one in which the directions are simple and easy to grasp, but when all is said and done, a game is easy or hard to learn according to the way in which the leader gives her directions. While most of the responsibility for making a game easy to learn falls back on the leader, nevertheless a fairly safe rule to follow is to choose games which require a minimum of directions.

Another safe rule is to look ahead and foresee the action of a game so as to anticipate any opportunities for rough play. Can you imagine a group of men and girls playing a game of "Dodge Ball," the object of which is to hit the legs of those in the center with a large ball? I saw a leader use that game with decidedly disastrous results. It is not quick, unexpected action that is dangerous in a game. "Merry-go-round" is full of such action, but with it there is a swing and a rhythm and a laugh that inevitably carries a group above and beyond the rough element.

The same can be said of races. We almost never use just plain running races for a group of men and women. But a race like the "Folding Chair Race," in which an entirely different element is brought in, namely, the folding chair, is sometimes the most successful event of an evening. Contestants occasionally fall down, but the thought in the mind of every one is not that a guest fell full-length on the floor but rather, "For pity's sake get up and get that folding chair down to the goal!"

But, you say, sometimes you just can't tell that a game is going to take a rough turn. That certainly is true, but in that event your move is to change the game at the first possible point that can be used as a transition to another game.

Have you seen a leader start a game that turned out to be either fearfully stupid, or almost started a riot because of its boisterous propensities? Sometimes I have seen a leader give up in a situation like that, and thereby admit that the game was a failure. As a result, she had a deadly struggle in drawing her group up again to an equally high plane of interest. But I have seen another leader who, when she saw what an utter failure a game was going to be, use it as a foundation for another game, the most foolish one she could think of. The transition was not technically perfect, but the effect on the guests was pluperfect. She was a real leader.

Quick transitions are hard, mighty hard, but they are positively necessary. It has almost as bad an effect on a group to stop a game outright because it is plainly rough, as it would have been to let it go on; so if it is in any way possible, change the game quickly rather than stop it. Better still, try to anticipate opportunities for rough play in the games you choose.

"Good Night, Ladies"

Do you feel highly gratified when, after your announcement that the party is over, some of your guests insist on having some more fun? If you are a human being, you do. But do you give in and let part of them play "just a few more games," while the rest are saying "Good night" and straggling homeward? Or have you tried the other method of closing a party in some definite way that will leave your guests with a very real, very tangible impression of having had a wonderful evening which they would have liked tremendously well to prolong? The "definite closing" can be one of your trump cards.

I have tried giving in to their request and letting them straggle out, group by group, and I have tried the other way of definitely closing a party with "Good Night, Ladies." To my mind there is no comparison between the two methods in the effect which they have on the minds of the guests. "Good Night, Ladies," sung with real feeling immediately following one of the very best

games of the evening, almost always creates the feeling,
"Well, we surely have had a good time. Time to go
home now." But when a party simply stops with nothing definite to mark the closing in the mind of the guest,
the enjoyment of the evening is vague and unfinished.
Of course, I do not mean that any one who lingers after
"Good Night, Ladies," is thrown out bodily! But the
party is over and all entertainment and all games are
over.

There is a very real point involved. If you have been
using the right kind of psychology your last game was
chosen for a definite purpose and you definitely worked
up to it. You have been watching reactions and you feel
the time to close an evening. It is not just a hit or miss
proposition but a vitally important part of your evening's plan, for a successful and timely close to a party
is without question worth the weight of your guests in
gold!

You, Again

And now, in conclusion, let us be personal. If you do
not thoroughly enjoy play and honestly can not educate
yourself in the real joy in play, do not try to be a
recreation leader. Your group reflects you and your attitude as surely as does a mirror. If you are leading
because you are paid to do so, if you are leading because
you like to feel that you are a leader, if you are tired, or
if you are bored, be sure that you cannot deceive your
guests for one minute.

If you are scared, that is another matter. No group
likes to see its leader frightened and not sure of herself,
but a leader who loves fun as much as any one of her

guests and who has the friendliest feeling toward every one of them, even if she has not as yet gained confidence in herself, has not much to fear in the matter of their taking advantage of her.

So, even though your stage-fright stays with you a long time, if at heart you are one with your guests, if your whole soul, your mind and your personality are put into your leadership, that leadership will inevitably and constantly become a bigger and more powerful factor in spreading the gospel of recreation.

INDEX